The Palgrave Kets de Vries Library

Manfred F. R. Kets de Vries, Distinguished Professor of Leadership and Development and Organizational Change at INSEAD, is one of the world's leading thinkers on leadership, coaching, and the application of clinical psychology to individual and organizational change.

Palgrave's professional business list operates at the interface between academic rigor and real-world implementation. Professor Kets de Vries's work exemplifies that perfect combination of intellectual depth and practical application and Palgrave is proud to bring almost a decade's worth of work together in the Palgrave Kets de Vries Library.

Manfred F. R. Kets de Vries

The Path to Authentic Leadership

Dancing with the Ouroboros

Manfred F. R. Kets de Vries
Kets De Vries Et Associees
Paris, France

ISSN 2730-7581   ISSN 2730-759X (electronic)
The Palgrave Kets de Vries Library
ISBN 978-3-031-04698-8   ISBN 978-3-031-04699-5 (eBook)
https://doi.org/10.1007/978-3-031-04699-5

© The Editor(s) (if applicable) and The Author(s), under exclusive licence to Springer Nature Switzerland AG 2023
This work is subject to copyright. All rights are solely and exclusively licensed by the Publisher, whether the whole or part of the material is concerned, specifically the rights of reprinting, reuse of illustrations, recitation, broadcasting, reproduction on microfilms or in any other physical way, and transmission or information storage and retrieval, electronic adaptation, computer software, or by similar or dissimilar methodology now known or hereafter developed.
The use of general descriptive names, registered names, trademarks, service marks, etc. in this publication does not imply, even in the absence of a specific statement, that such names are exempt from the relevant protective laws and regulations and therefore free for general use.
The publisher, the authors and the editors are safe to assume that the advice and information in this book are believed to be true and accurate at the date of publication. Neither the publisher nor the authors or the editors give a warranty, expressed or implied, with respect to the material contained herein or for any errors or omissions that may have been made. The publisher remains neutral with regard to jurisdictional claims in published maps and institutional affiliations.

This Palgrave Macmillan imprint is published by the registered company Springer Nature Switzerland AG.
The registered company address is: Gewerbestrasse 11, 6330 Cham, Switzerland

Contents

1 **Introduction: Dancing with the Ouroboros** 1
  Time, Rebirth, and the Ouroboros 1
  Being Twice Born 3
  Our Character Armor 5
  The Red Thread 6
  Spinning Our Fate 11

2 **Covid and the Seven Deadly Sins** 13
  Leadership Virtues Post Pandemic 19

3 **Evil: Reality and Imagination** 21
  The Ambiguity of Evil 23
    Obedience to Authority 24
  Group Dynamics 26
  The Dark Psyche 28
    Nurture and Nature 28
  Preventing Evil 29
    Mental Acrobatics 30
    What Is Moral? 30
    Creating a Secure Base 32

    Don't Be a Bystander   36
    Societal Considerations   36
    Avoiding the Darkness   38

4   The Psychology of White-Collar Criminals   41
Introduction   41
The Fraud Triangle   44
The People Equation   46
    The Greed Factor   46
    Low Behavioral Self-Control   47
    Narcissistic Disposition   47
    Corporate Psychopathy   48
    Neuro-criminology   49
Ways of Prevention   49
    Corporate Culture   51
    Leadership Development   51
    Entry and Exit   52
    Control Systems   52
The Perfect Crime   52

5   The Dance Macabre of Shame   55
Shame and the Human Condition   56
    Shame vs. Guilt   58
    An Evolutionary Perspective   58
    The Psychological Perspective   59
Overcoming Shame   60
A Master Emotion   66

6   Catching the Thief of Time: The Perils of Procrastination   67
Introduction   67
The Procrastinator Test   68
Contributing Variables to Procrastination   69
Character Types   71
Behavioral Recommendations   72
    Too Big a Task   73
    Lack of Self-Control   73

	Time Management	74
	Recognize Busyness	74
	Have Some Fun	75
	What's Happening Under the Surface?	75
	Perfectionism	75
	A Highly Critical Superego	77
7	**The Inner Theater of the Super-Rich**	81
	Introduction	81
	Becoming a Billionaire	83
	The Inner Theater	84
	The Dark Dyad Revisited	89
	Managing Wealth	91
8	**To Hell with Charisma**	93
	Introduction	93
	The Darker Side of Charisma	95
	Charisma and Transference	98
	A Lack of Philosopher-Kings	99
	The Importance of Civil Education	101
9	**Transformation Challenges**	105
10	**Creating Emotionally Intelligent Organizations**	115
11	**Magic and Management**	123
	Historical Musings	124
	The Allure of Pseudoscience	125
	The Need to Manage Uncertainty	126
	Singularity and Lack of Specificity	127
	Human Gullibility	127
	Astrology's Darker Side	129
	A More Empowered Way to Go Through Life	129

| 12 | Kōans as Agents of Change | 133 |

Negative Capability 133
Ambiguity in Action 134
What Had Happened? 135
Opening the Mind Through Not-Knowing 136
Preventing Early Closure and Allowing for Ambiguity 138
Wrestling with Kōans 139
Learning, Unlearning, and Relearning 143
Getting You, the Reader, More Stuck 146
Ending the Circle 149

| 13 | Concluding Remarks | 151 |

The Transformative Self 151
Creative Destruction 155

Index 159

About the Author

Manfred F. R. Kets de Vries brings a different view to the much-studied subjects of leadership and the psychological dimensions of individual and organizational change. Bringing to bear his knowledge and experience of economics (Econ. Drs., University of Amsterdam), management (ITP, MBA, and DBA, Harvard Business School), and psychoanalysis (Membership Canadian Psychoanalytic Society, Paris Psychoanalytic Society, and the International Psychoanalytic Association), he explores the interface between management science, psychoanalysis, developmental psychology, evolutionary psychology, neuroscience, psychotherapy, executive coaching, and management consulting. His specific areas of interest are leadership (the "bright" and "dark" sides), entrepreneurship, career dynamics, talent management, family business, cross-cultural management, succession planning, organizational and individual stress, C-suite team building, executive coaching, organizational development, transformation management, and management consulting.

As the Distinguished Clinical Professor of Leadership Development and Organizational Change at INSEAD, he is Program Director of INSEAD's top management program, "The Challenge of Leadership: Creating Reflective Leaders," and the Founder of INSEAD's Executive Master Program in Change Management. He has also been the founder of INSEAD's Global Leadership Center. Furthermore, he has been a world-renowned pioneer in team coaching. As an educator, he has received INSEAD's distinguished MBA teacher award six times. He has held professorships at McGill University, the École des Hautes Études Commerciales, the European School for Management and Technology (ESMT), and the Harvard Business School. He has lectured at management institutions around the world. The *Financial Times, Le Capital, Wirtschaftswoche*, and *The Economist* have rated Manfred Kets de Vries among the world's leading management thinkers and among the most influential contributors to human resource management.

Kets de Vries is the author, co-author, or editor of more than 50 books, including *The Neurotic Organization; Organizational Paradoxes; Struggling with the Demon: Perspectives on Individual and Organizational Irrationality; Leaders, Fools and Impostors; Life and Death in the Executive Fast Lane; Prisoners of Leadership; The Leadership Mystique; The Happiness Equation; Are Leaders Made or Are They Born?: The Case of Alexander the Great; The New Russian Business Elite; Leadership by Terror: Finding Shaka Zulu in the Attic; The Leader on the Couch; The Family Business on the Couch; Sex, Money, Happiness, and Death: The Quest for Authenticity, Reflections on Leadership and Character; Reflections on Leadership and Career; Reflections on Organizations; The Coaching Kaleidoscope; The Hedgehog Effect: The Secrets of High Performance Teams; Mindful Leadership Coaching: Journeys into the Interior; You Will Meet a Tall Dark Stranger: Executive Coaching Challenges; Telling Fairy Tales in the Boardroom: How to Make Sure Your Organization Lives Happily Ever After; Riding the Leadership Roller Coaster: A Psychological Observer's Guide; Down the Rabbit Hole of Leadership: Leadership Pathology of Everyday Life; The CEO Whisperer: Meditations on Leaders, Life and Change; Quo Vadis: The Existential Challenges of Leaders; Leadership Unhinged: Essays on the Ugly, the Bad, and the Weird; Leading Wisely: Becoming a Reflective Leader in Turbulent Times;* and *The Daily Perils of Executive Life: How to Survive When Dancing on Quicksand.* Furthermore, he has designed various 360-degree feedback instruments, including the widely used *Global Executive Leadership Mirror* and the *Organizational Culture Audit.*

In addition, Kets de Vries has published more than 400 academic papers as chapters in books and as articles. He has also written approximately 100 case studies, including seven that received the Best Case of the Year award. Furthermore, he has written hundreds of mini articles (blogs) for the Harvard Business Review, INSEAD Knowledge, and other digital outlets. He is also a regular writer for various magazines. His work has been featured in such publications as *The New York Times*, *The Wall Street Journal*, the *Los Angeles Times*, *Fortune*, *Business Week*, *The Economist*, the *Financial Times*, and the *Harvard Business Review*. His books and articles have been translated into more than thirty languages.

Furthermore, Kets de Vries is a member of seventeen editorial boards and is a Fellow of the Academy of Management. In addition, he is on the board of a number of charitable organizations. He is also a founding member of the International Society for the Psychoanalytic Study of Organizations (ISPSO), which has honored him as a lifetime member. In addition, Kets de Vries is the first non-US recipient of the International Leadership Association Lifetime Achievement Award for his contributions to leadership research and development (being considered one of the world's founding professionals in the development of leadership as a field and discipline). He received a Lifetime Achievement Award from Germany for his advancement of executive education. The American Psychological Association has honored him with the "Harry and Miriam Levinson Award" for his contributions to Organizational Consultation. Furthermore, he is the recipient of the "Freud Memorial Award" for his work to further the interface between management and psychoanalysis. In addition, he has also received the "Vision of Excellence Award" from the Harvard Institute of Coaching. Kets de Vries is the first beneficiary of INSEAD's Dominique Héau Award for "Inspiring Educational Excellence." He is also the recipient of three honorary doctorates. The Dutch government has made him an Officer in the Order of Oranje Nassau.

Kets de Vries works as a consultant on organizational design/transformation and strategic human resource management for companies worldwide. As an educator and consultant, he has worked in more than forty countries. In his role as a consultant, he is also the founder-chairman of the Kets de Vries Institute (KDVI), a boutique global strategic leadership development consulting firm with associates worldwide (www.kdvi.com).

About the Author

Kets de Vries was the first fly fisherman in Outer Mongolia (at the time, becoming the world record holder of the Siberian hucho taimen). He is a member of New York's Explorers Club. In his spare time, he can be found in the rainforests or savannas of Central and Southern Africa, the Siberian taiga, the Ussuri Krai, Kamchatka, the Pamir, and Altai Mountains, Arnhemland, or within the Arctic Circle.

1

Introduction: Dancing with the Ouroboros

It is not more surprising to be born twice than once; everything in nature is resurrection.
—*Voltaire*

It is said of the ouroboros that he slays himself and brings himself to life, fertilizes himself and gives birth to himself.
—*Carl Jung*

Time, Rebirth, and the Ouroboros

What's the ouroboros? And why should we be interested in this strange image of a serpent eating its own tail in this collection of essays on authentic leadership?

In answering these questions, let's begin by adopting an etymological perspective. The term "ouroboros" originates from the Greek *oura* meaning "tail" and *boros* signifying "eating," thus referring to "he who eats his tail." Its imagery has a very long history. In fact, the earliest record of this image appeared in the thirteenth century BC on a golden shrine in the tomb of the Egyptian king Tutankhamen. It was used to depict the way the ancient

Egyptians understood time. To them, time wasn't seen as a linear process. On the contrary, it was portrayed as a series of repetitive cycles, very much based on the imagery of the flooding of the Nile or the journey of the sun. Thus, the ouroboros became symbolic of the cycle of life, death, and rebirth. To be more specific, the ancient Egyptians already recognized how nature created life out of destruction. And as the ouroboros was a symbol without a beginning or end, it also signified a break with the linear, and instead focused on the cyclical. No wonder that the loop represented by the ouroboros was bound to the concept of time, the circle being symbolic of the finite and infinite. In fact, the current mathematical symbol for infinity may have been derived from a variant of the classic representation of the ouroboros.

The ouroboros imagery helps us to reconsider how to look at our lives. It presents us with an eternal cycle of destruction and re-creation. Or as the well-known mythologist Joseph Campbell would say, "Life lives on life. This is the sense of the symbol of the ouroboros, the serpent biting its tail. Everything that lives, lives on the death of something else. Your own body will be food for something else. Anyone who denies this, anyone who holds back, is out of order. Death is an act of giving."

At this stage of my life, the symbolic nature of the ouroboros has increased in significance. Drawing on the life cycle theory as developed by one of my former teachers, the psychoanalyst Erik Erikson, I have now reached that later stage in life he painted by using the polarity of integrity versus despair. To Erikson, integrity refers to our ability to look back at our life with a sense of accomplishment and fulfillment—to be satisfied with what we have achieved. It alludes to a sense of feeling whole, of being at peace with ourselves. Alternatively, on the other side of the coin, we find despair, conveyed by a sense of bitterness and regret—the feeling of having led a wasted life. This sense of despair also refers to a need to ruminate over mistakes made, not to mention falling into the abyss of depression. Thus, at this integrity-versus-despair stage of life, we might be asking ourselves whether we have led a meaningful, satisfying life. We may have doubts about the choices we've made. Given the way we have lived our lives, we could well question whether we let go of other opportunities. In short, could we have made better choices?

In light of the human condition, having such feelings is inevitable. Doubts about the choices we have made is all too human. And transcending these doubts will be quite a challenge. However, instead of torturing ourselves about the choices we've made, wouldn't it be much wiser to ask ourselves whether our choices have been "good enough"? Have our choices been satisfactory? After all, searching for perfection is an invitation to misery. Isn't it true that the wise strive to do their best, while the foolish strive for perfection? We can only hope that at the end of our days, we have come to accept that we did the best we could; that whatever we did, made for a well-lived life. Only by feeling good enough—not in a search for perfection—can we set ourselves free.

Being Twice Born

But if feeling "good enough" isn't an option, the imagery of the ouroboros can be helpful. If we don't feel good in our skin, taking its symbolism as a guideline, we can always try to reinvent ourselves. We can strive for a "rebirth," if only symbolically. In fact, at the beginning of the twentieth century, the Harvard psychologist and philosopher William James already made a distinction between people who were "once-born" and "twice-born." According to James, "once-borns" are individuals who do not stray from the straight and narrow. They are tied to familiar territory where they have always felt comfortable. Some of them, however, during their life's journey, may have become spiritually and intellectually challenged. When faced with unexpected adversity, such as dramatic life crises, they could become "reborn." These "twice-borns"—people who have undergone an experience of fundamental, moral, and spiritual upheaval (a near-death experience would be the most dramatic example)—may have the courage to transcend their self-limitations. Given what they have experienced, they may see it as necessary to make dramatic changes to their lives.

But that's not to say that gradual or incremental change cannot have its advantages. Transition does not always require great drama. We do not necessarily have to look death in the face. Sometimes, changing our orientation to the world may come about when small frustrations gradually build up, eventually becoming unbearable. And that might be the moment that prepares some people for a major change. Even though in these situations it may take much more time for meaningful change to occur, it provides the comfort of getting where we want to go in a more expectable and safe manner. And even though the process may only be an incremental one, by taking small steps we may also be able to break our dysfunctional habits, to build new ones that will help us to better deal with future challenges. Unfortunately, if we choose to take this route, there will always be the chance that we may get stuck in purgatory. It could very well be that each small step forward will be quickly nullified by everything else that is wrong with our lives. If that's the case, then incrementalism isn't going to be the answer.

In contrast, affected by a dramatic life experience, twice-borns have come to realize that their perspective on life is no longer good enough. Whatever happened, it has created a feeling of imbalance. It makes them prepared to sacrifice their present dissatisfied self for a future, more hopeful self. And even though they may resist making the necessary changes, at the same time, they may also be looking forward to entering a new version of life. It is all part of this "twice-born" process.

By undertaking such a journey, these twice-borns may be able to attain a greater sense of authenticity, integrating the conscious and the unconscious parts of their psyche. Subjecting themselves to this kind of psychological labor will contribute to a greater awareness of who they truly are. And by acknowledging the different aspects of themselves—including their flaws and imperfections—they may be able to reach a level of self-actualization that otherwise they would never have reached. This is the kind of integration that contributes to greater inner peace. In other words, what we can observe is how twice-born people actively use difficult changes in their external life to come to peace with their inner demons. They not only recognize their flaws but also try to use this knowledge to build a more integrated self. It is this transformation of the self that leads to a reaffirmation of life.

Often, twice-born people have made heroic efforts to reinvent themselves because they have realized that if they don't embark on change, they might descend into a state of living death. It is what made them decide to escape their self-imposed mental prisons. They want to free themselves from whatever purgatory they're finding themselves in. In fact, it could very well be that human beings may need to go through purgatory to experience life to its fullest. As the German philosopher Friedrich Nietzsche said in *Thus Spoke Zarathustra*, "You must be ready to burn yourself in your own flame; how could you rise anew if you have not first become ashes?"[1] Afterwards, due to these experiences, these "twice-borns" may discover that they have been given a new lease of life. The ability to reinvent themselves changes the way they will relate to other people and the world at large.

Our Character Armor

Referring to the ability to reinvent ourselves, we should always keep in mind that human beings tend to be "lazy" creatures. During our journey through life—acquiring our various behavior patterns—we become increasingly reluctant to change. In fact, we prefer to stick to our well-tried-out routines. Gradually, as time has gone by, we have developed what can be described as a character armor.[2] We have become increasingly more rigid in the way we are functioning. After all, compared to the speed of our physical birth, our psychological birth will take much more time. Developing our unique personality characteristics doesn't happen overnight. It tends to be a gradual, interactive process of development influenced by parents, other family members, teachers, and various important people who create significant life experiences. These personality characteristics will very much determine who we are; how we behave; and how we act. And what's more, during this "incubation" process, the behavior patterns that we acquire will be written into the structure of our brain. Naturally, this brain structure will undergo its most profound development and growth at the earliest stages of our lives—a period when we are much more malleable.

---

[1] Friedrich Nietzsche (2000). *Basic Writings of Nietzsche* (Modern Library Classics). New York: Modern Library.
[2] Wilhelm Reich (1975). *Character Analysis*, 5th enlarged edition, New York: Farrar Publishing.

Fortunately, our character isn't written in stone. Important as early developmental processes may be, they're only part of what makes us who we are. Salient experiences that we will have during our life's journey will also leave their stamp. The more dramatic, the more impactful these experiences are, the more they will affect us. Tragically, desperation often becomes the raw material that helps us change. Thus, even though we may be less malleable in comparison to when we were young, change is always possible. We can always attain some kind of "second birth." In other words, once our brain has developed, it is still capable of substantial change even in adult life.

As mentioned before, for the twice-borns, such a "rebirth" will be a transition to a parallel or alternative perspective. Other "rebirths" may take the form of a "peak experience" of only momentary significance, possibly only temporarily evoked by the circumstances. But even such a temporary "rebirth" could contribute to greater insight about ourselves, making for a greater sense of individuation. We might become more our own person, with our own beliefs and our own ideals. Of course, what's also implied is that we are trying to make a change to the structure of our brains. It explains why change can be so very hard—and why the process can take such a long time. After all, it is not easy to make changes to the character armor that we have constructed.

The Red Thread

The reason for my interest in being once-born or twice-born is that during my life I have had several near-death experiences that have affected me profoundly. Obviously, apart from the physical impact caused by these experiences, these incidents also have had a psychological impact. It led me to question the meaning of my existence—to ask myself what makes life worth living. And as is to be expected, while dwelling in the dungeons of my mind, it can be a real challenge to find a way out—to create an alternative universe. Frankly speaking, these experiences have very much affected my life's trajectory. On various occasions, they have motivated me in trying to reinvent myself. This drive to reinvent myself also explains why I am so intrigued by the symbolism represented by the ouroboros.

Taking as example only my professional identity, I have been somewhat of a shapeshifter, pursuing various roles in life, including being an engineer, economist, professor of management, researcher, psychoanalyst/therapist, administrator, management consultant, executive coach, and author.

Despite these various work identities, eventually the red thread running through these various shapes has been a *Weltanschauung* colored by a psychodynamic-systemic lens. As a psychoanalyst, I have been a disciple of what Sigmund Freud describes as the "impossible profession." In that respect, I may also have taken on something of a shamanistic identity. After all—notwithstanding its mystical nature—shamanism can be considered the origin of all psychotherapies. Throughout human history, it has been the shamans who would bridge the world of the living and the world of the spirits. Also, it has been the shamans who ensured that the right ceremonies would be enacted in the right way to put the world to rights. Furthermore, it has been the shamans who took on the role of explorers of the magnificent hidden universe that lies beyond this visible one. In that respect, it has been the shamans who served as brokers, searching for another dimension of seeing.

Thus, as a shaman in my own right, my life-goal has always been to help leaders to become more effective and humane—to create leaders who want their constituencies to flourish. In other words, in my work I have always tried to create the kinds of leaders who desire to get the best out of their people. I am referring to leaders who possess a solid dose of humility, authenticity, trustworthiness, empathy, and compassion—leaders who can withstand the siren's song of hubris—not the kinds of leaders looking just out for number one. And to make this happen—taking a "micro" level perspective—in my dealings with them I have always tried to "simulate" the kinds of experiences that have impact. I have always tried to create learning communities that would enable the participants to learn from each other. And in doing so, I have always tried to transform these learning communities into incubation centers for personal change. At the same time, taking more of a "macro" perspective, I have always seen it as my life's task to bring the human dimension back into the organization—to create the kinds of organizations that have a human quality—that become the best places to work. In addition, I have also tried to bring these ideas into the political sphere. In other words, increasingly I have seen as part of my agenda to do everything in my power to prevent the rise of pathological leadership. And I am not alone in being conscious of the danger represented by these people, given the large stage on which these people operate.

I have always asked myself why some people in leadership positions abuse the power that comes with the job, while others don't. What distinguishes the Mugabes and the Mandelas of this world? Why did a "psychologically challenged" person such as Donald Trump succeed in becoming the president of the United States? How is it imaginable that a person like Jair Bolsonaro of Brazil would get away with what he does, given his many very dangerous idiocracies? How is it possible that people like President Alexander Lukashenko of Belarus or General Min Aung Hlaing of Myanmar can continue to terrorize their people? And what about the disastrous war in the Ukraine, initiated by President Vladimir Putin? In fact, why do some leaders rise to the light while others lead their people into darkness?[3] In this context, Lord Acton's words of "power corrupts, and absolute power corrupts absolutely" have often been quoted. Unquestionably, when the sirens of power beckon, many people cannot resist its call. But do these people realize how in their strivings for self-aggrandizement they're making life hell for others?

I have always seen it as my mandate to help people become better than they think they can be—a task that, as an educator, I take very seriously. I have always sought to help people actualize their dreams about the future—to turn these dreams into a reality—a part of this self-imposed mandate. To enable this to happen, what's often needed is to have these people regain the playfulness that they once possessed, a quality that they may have left behind during their life's journey. And by resorting to this long-lost playfulness, they might even be able to make the ouroboros dance.

Unfortunately, in the world we live in, the kind of leadership that gets the best out of people is rare. There are very few leaders who encourage their constituencies to be the best that they can be. Far from it, as I have suggested, in too many countries, what we can observe is more of a leadership meltdown. Too many of the world's political leaders are exhibiting

---

[3] Manfred F. R. Kets de Vries (2021). *Leadership Unhinged: Essays on the Ugly, the Bad, and the Weird*. London: Palgrave.

behavior patterns that should be excised from the leadership equation. Too many of these populist-demagogue leaders have created worlds of make-believe, leading their people astray.[4] All too often, in this age of greed, paranoia, anxiety, and depression, short-term expediency prevails, while bold, imaginative leadership is sorely missing. Twice-born thinking is notable by its absence.

In my work with leaders, however, I have not given up hope. I sincerely wish that a new generation of leaders will rise to the challenge. And in a small way, I am prepared to do all I can to make it happen. I realize, however, that to enable this to happen it will be necessary for the leaders of the future to acquire a solid dose of self-knowledge. They will need to be able to recognize their strengths and weaknesses. They will need to understand the darker side of leadership. And as I mentioned before, to arrive at such a degree of self-understanding will require the ability to deal with their inner demons. It implies a willingness to accept the irrationality within. After all, a *sine qua non* in creating more effective leaders is to make them realize that they are not rational decision makers—that much of their behavior is out-of-awareness—that they may have many blind spots that require attention. And to overcome their inner demons, they may even have to reinvent themselves. They may have to pay attention to the symbolism offered by the ouroboros.

Too many leaders aren't familiar with the statement written above the Temple of Apollo in ancient Delphi: "Know thyself." And this observation is as true today as it was in those bygone times. In fact, the most exemplary recent political leader, Nelson Mandela, once said, "You can never have an impact on society if you have not changed yourself." If we want to develop more effective leaders, we must start with ourselves. But as I have discovered, to paraphrase Goethe, what is often hardest to see is what is right in front of your eyes.

Through my teaching and writing, I have always tried to help people with new beginnings. I have always tried to create "aha" experiences for my students that could turn into tipping points for change. I have always tried to help people to understand what they're all about. It explains my use of

---

[4] Manfred F. R. Kets de Vries (2021). *Leadership Unhinged: Essays on the Ugly, the Bad, and the Weird*. London: Palgrave.

the symbolism of the ouroboros to tie together the disparate essays in this book. Despite the different nature of these essays, in the various chapters that make up this book, the cycle of destruction and creation is always to be found. Dualities, instances of opposition and contrasts, permeate each of these essays. Keeping the ouroboros symbolism in mind, each essay also relates to some form of transformation. In addition, what also ties these various essays together is the fact that they were written as a response to questions raised by my students. In a way, each essay can be looked at as an answer to my not-knowing—and my attempts to try to know.

Starting with the first essay that deals with the seven deadly sins—a concept introduced by the early Christian church fathers—I take another look at these sins in the context of the pandemic. Despite the horrendous destructiveness of Covid-19, this essay contains the hope that the pandemic can also become a catalyst for constructive transformative processes. Moving on to the next essay, I illuminate how the symbolism of the ouroboros provides us with greater insights about the horrors of evil. There I ponder the question of what motivates people to enter this darkness. And in this context, I also try in the next essay to elaborate on this point by analyzing a special category of evil doers: white-collar criminals. Why, for all appearances' sake, do quite normal human beings become transformed in such a way as to participate in criminal activities? What makes them act in this way?

The ouroboros effect is also applicable to the two essays that follow, which explore shame and procrastination. Again, I point out that these behavior patterns are part of this macabre dance relating to destruction and creation. Subsequently, in the next essay—taking more of a transformative view—I put the inner theater of the super-rich under the microscope. I raise the question of what makes these people different from the general population. What has contributed to making them the kinds of people that they are? What led to their transformation? And what can be said about their darker side? In the following essay, again within the context of destruction and creation, I make several observations about the nature of charisma. Although charisma can be transformative, in many instances, charismatic leaders can also be extremely destructive.

Then, in the following two chapters, I look closely at the question of how to transform organizations. There the focus is not only on the conundrum of creating emotionally intelligent organizations, but also on the forces that block these kinds of transformations. To continue this dance between destruction and creation, one of the final essays in this book deals with the imaginary, transformative power of magic. It points out how magic can be used for the wrong purposes; how it can lead to inappropriate decision-making. The last chapter in this book pertains to the transformative power of kōans, these paradoxical riddles to be meditated upon in Zen Buddhism. In this particular chapter, I try to demonstrate the inadequacy of logical reasoning and how transcending rationality can turn out to be quite rational. I also point out how intuitive processes can be helpful when trying to overcome not-knowing. Finally, in the summing up, I compare the ouroboros symbolism with the pictogram of the phoenix—how to rise from the ashes. Again, it is a reminder that things cannot remain the same forever—that there will be times when we need to break with the past. Or to quote the Italian writer Giuseppe Tomasi di Lampedusa from his famous novel *Il Gattopardo* [*The Leopard*], "If you want things to stay as they are, things will have to change."

Spinning Our Fate

As a way of recapitulating this introduction, we all recognize that the most important parts of the natural order are birth and death. All of us try to make the best of the life that's been given to us. And during our life's trajectory, health, happiness, and success will play important parts. Whether these desires are achieved is another matter. Although we have a degree of control on how our life unfolds, there is also the matter of fate.

To give our life's trajectory greater meaning, the Ancient Greeks created deities that would determine their fate. To have real figures determining important moments in this journey would give greater clarity to what the cycle of life would be all about. These Fates or Moirai would be represented in the form of three very old women who would spin the threads of our lives. They assigned individual destinies to mortals at birth, essentially standing for birth, life, and death. They would ensure that every mortal would live out their destiny as it was assigned to them by the laws of the universe. And the names of these Moirai were Clotho (the Spinner), Lachesis (the Allotter), and Atropos (the Inflexible). Clotho spun the thread of life onto her spindle. Lachesis measured the thread of life allotted to each person with her measuring rod. Atropos was the cutter of the thread of life, choosing the manner of each person's death.

Even though the three Fates are no longer part of our contemporary reality, symbolically they continue to do their work. And the outcome is very much determined by nature and nurture, as well as serendipity. Fortunately, despite the immovable forces of destiny—not knowing what fate has waiting for us—hope remains. That's the gift of the ouroboros, given its cyclical nature. As Fyodor Dostoyevsky said very astutely, "To live without hope is to cease to live." After all, hope will always be a powerful force. Hope is important because it can make the present moment less difficult to bear. Or to quote the Roman statesman Cicero, "When there is life, there is hope." After all, everything that is done in this world is driven by hope. And all of us need hope—young or old, strong or weak, rich or poor. In fact, there is no medicine like hope, no incentive so great, and no tonic so powerful as the expectation of something better tomorrow. It makes hope the anchor of our souls, dwelling in our dreams, catching our imagination. And it is hope that gives us the courage to turn our dreams into reality. Frankly speaking, if we believe that tomorrow will be better, we can bear whatever hardship we experience today. It is our hopes, not our hurts, that shape our future. And the simple act of living with hope—the daily effort to have a positive impact in the world—makes the days left to us by the Fates more precious and meaningful.

My hope is that through my work with people—even though it may be wishful thinking—I will leave the world a tiny bit better than when I got here. And that's a desire that applies to all of us. To create a better world for our children, all of us should entertain such thoughts. Or to quote the French scientist Marie Curie: "You cannot hope to build a better world without improving the individuals. To that end, each of us must work for his own improvement and, at the same time, share a general responsibility for all humanity, our particular duty being to aid those to whom we think we can be most useful."

2

Covid and the Seven Deadly Sins

All the world's a stage, and all the men and women merely players: they have their exits and their entrances; and one man in his time plays many parts, his acts being seven ages.
—*William Shakespeare*

We are rarely proud when we are alone.
—*Voltaire*

Thinking about hope, I was recently admiring the series of prints entitled "The Seven Deadly Sins" by the sixteenth-century Dutch artist Peter Bruegel the Elder. Each print features a central image that represents one of the seven sins. However, it's worth noting that these deadly sins have a long history that extends well before Bruegel's time. First highlighted in the sixth century by Pope Gregory I and later elaborated on in the thirteenth century by Saint Thomas Aquinas, they were discussed in treatises and depicted in paintings and sculpture decorations on Catholic churches, as well as in old textbooks. The standard list of vices included pride, greed, wrath, envy, lust, gluttony, and sloth—behavior patterns that were thought to contribute to immoral behavior. This classification originated

© The Author(s), under exclusive license to Springer Nature Switzerland AG 2023
M. F. R. Kets de Vries, *The Path to Authentic Leadership*, The Palgrave Kets de Vries Library, https://doi.org/10.1007/978-3-031-04699-5_2

with the early Christian hermits referred to as the desert fathers who practiced asceticism in the Egyptian desert. As a matter of fact, it was the hermit Evagrius the Solitary, one of the most influential theologians of the late fourth-century church, who first identified the seven or eight evil spirits that people needed to overcome.

While looking at these prints, I was also reminded of the drawings of Sandro Botticelli, the famous Italian painter of the early Renaissance. He very graphically illustrated the *Inferno* of Dante Alighieri's *The Divine Comedy*. In his writings, Dante presented these capital sins as perverse or corrupt versions of love. For example, lust, gluttony, and greed were portrayed as excessive love of good things. Wrath, envy, and pride were depicted as perverted love or harm toward others. The sole exception to these "perversions" was sloth, the sin of letting go of responsibilities, and by extension a deficiency of love.

Coincidentally, very soon after I had been looking at these engravings, a friend sent me a cartoon which portrayed a man standing in his office pointing at a blackboard that showed an organization chart that listed these seven sins with the added comment *"Welcome aboard Manfred. Where do you see yourself in the general scheme of things?"*

Where do I see myself? Certainly, I fit somewhere. After all, these cravings are part of the human condition and holiness is an illusion. It is important to note that what constitutes each of these as a sin is the indulgence in excess. Clearly, the notion of seven deadly sins originated from the belief that excessive application of our passions becomes sinful or immoral. On the other hand, could circumstantial factors contribute to this excess? For example, has the present pandemic affected the way these deadly sins are manifested?

Take lust as an example. Has the pandemic affected people's desire and subsequently sex life? Needless to say, it is hard to generalize about this subject. Our sex life very much depends on our sexual fantasies, our partner, the quality and the duration of a marriage, whether there are children in such a relationship, and many other factors. A relatively common scenario during pre-pandemic times would be a long-term couple living parallel lives, each busy with their many commitments. However, the pandemic-related lockdowns might have offered a much-needed break from their mutual busyness. In fact, being stuck at home together could have transformed into a temporary honeymoon. As the pandemic forced many couples to slow down, it might have given them the opportunity to take more time to reconnect and to spend more intimate moments together. In other words, during the beginning of the lockdown, it may have resulted in a short uptake in their sex life. All good things, however, come to an end. For many of these couples, as time went by and due to persistent worries, be they financial, health or otherwise, their sexual appetite might have deteriorated. Furthermore, the ever-present dangers of other Covid-19-specific concerns might have added to an atmosphere of uncertainty and fear, contributing to depressive reactions—which is contrary to the state of mind needed for lust. Additionally, spending long uninterrupted periods of time with another person in a restrained environment wouldn't be exactly the kind of ambience that evoked lustful thoughts.

What about another vice like gluttony? Since the pandemic, the waistline of many people seemed to have expanded. According to one study, since the start of the pandemic, people's weight has steadily increased by about 1.5 pounds per month.[1] If so, given the duration of the pandemic, and based on the projections of this study, many people would have become seriously overweight or even obese. In fact, overeating could well be driven by an effort to compensate for the anxiety and fears due to Covid-19. In stressful times, people often resort to unhealthy coping mechanisms. In particular, the consumption of sweetened beverages and other sugary snack foods appeared to have gone up. Another factor contributing to weight gain might have been the consumption of greater amounts of alcohol. And by combining these behaviors with a lack of physical activity due to the closing of gyms and offices, weight gain might have become inevitable. Thus, by summing up all these factors, the pandemic may have pushed people toward gluttony, behaviors that, in the long run, would contribute to serious health problems such as high blood pressure, heart disease, and diabetes.

---

[1] https://www.health.harvard.edu/staying-healthy/pandemic-weight-gain-not-your-imagination; https://www.healthline.com/health-news/61-percent-of-americans-say-they-gained-weight-during-the-pandemic

Sadly speaking, greed has been very much alive and well during these pandemic times. While Covid-19 has taken a terrible toll on millions of people across the globe, it has also been an opportunity for the wealthy to further enrich themselves, with prime examples being Amazon founder Jeff Bezos and Tesla founder Elon Musk. Over the course of the initial year of the pandemic, they have added tens of billions of dollars to their already bloated fortunes with soaring stock market valuations. As the Federal Reserve has kept interest rates at incredibly low levels, borrowing money has become extremely easy, thereby inducing a demand for shares on stock exchanges. And as far as specific industries are concerned, greed has been particularly prominent within pharmaceutical companies. While many of them have been lauded for finding a vaccine against Covid-19, we shouldn't forget that, after discovering an antidote, many have sold virtually their entire stock to the richer countries. In fact, doing so helped them to gain sky-high profit margins and share prices. At the same time, however, these companies have tried to block attempts led by developing countries to temporarily waive patents on their vaccines. They seemed to have forgotten that governments not only financed much of the basic research for the antidote but had also provided substantial upfront funds to bring the vaccines to market. But despite these substantial governmental contributions, many pharmaceutical companies would claim that a patent waiver would hurt "incentives" for innovation. If these companies would be able to look beyond profit—if all the vaccines would be distributed equitably—most of the world could be vaccinated much quicker, effectively ending the pandemic. After all, the only way to end the pandemic is to immunize enough people worldwide. The slogan "no one is safe until we are all safe" captured the epidemiological reality that the world is facing—and the reality of the devastating impact of the greed factor. Unfortunately, it seemed that too many of these pharmaceutical companies have been focused primarily on earnings, and not on global health.

Let's move on to wrath, or, to use a more familiar term, anger. The pandemic presented many people with unprecedented challenges. Covid-19 created much disruption to their normal life, creating feelings of great uncertainty regarding the future. As a reaction to these forces beyond their control, many of them would become extremely angry about their current situation. Furthermore, even though social isolation had been necessary to keep the virus at bay, it had also prevented people from social interaction—a very basic human need. Many people lost a sense of normality, routine, and contact with their family and friends. As many of them were struggling with a range of negative experiences and emotions, wrath or anger became a major outlet for their frustrations. In fact, anger signals not only that we feel threatened, but also that we are suffering. As a way of dealing with feelings of helplessness and distress, some people would express their wrath in the form of domestic violence and abuse. What also should be added is that these expressions of anger might only have been the tip of the iceberg, concealing other hidden emotions such as depressive reactions beneath the feelings of anger.

Moving on to sloth, much has been written on the changes in people's working habits due to the pandemic.[2] Since the beginning of the pandemic, many people were forced to adjust to new ways of working. This "new normal," however, would present itself with its own set of challenges. Many people were wondering, while working at home, how to accurately "anchor" their productivity. How could they be sure that they were doing a good job? And for people who were new to working from home, it might have been difficult to adjust to distance working. This adjustment would be especially difficult if they also were carrying the responsibility of schooling their children from home. Not having concrete anchor points (work vs. personal life space) would make some of these people think that every moment at home in lockdown should be spent working. If not, they might berate themselves for not using every moment at home productively. In fact, they might feel guilty when they would engage in various forms of "cyberloafing"—scrolling through social media or browse-shopping online, particularly in between big tasks at work. However, doing so might have been a good way to relax and to reinvigorate their brains. They may not have realized that what they were doing would be very similar to having a chat at the coffee shop at the office or a working lunch with their colleagues. Indeed, these guilt feelings about "laziness" would quite often be out of place. However, what shouldn't be underestimated is that for many

---

[2] Manfred F. R. Kets de Vries (2020). *Journeys into Coronavirus Land: Lessons from the Pandemic.* London: KDVI Press.

people, these tumultuous times sparked feelings of frustration, anxiety, uncertainty, anger, and grief, a prescription for feeling (and being) unproductive. Consequently, despite the possible benefits of working at home, it would be unrealistic to expect that everyone could keep up with one hundred percent of the workload or the level of productivity that they once sustained pre-pandemic. There would be some people who experienced mental health problems and depressive reactions. Consequently, due to lower levels of energy, they might not be as productive as they would like to have been, making feelings of slovenliness even more of a reality. No wonder that the "Great Resignation" or the "Big Quit," meaning the large number of employees voluntarily resigning from jobs, has become a reality for many companies.

Of course, among the list of vices we should not forget is envy, a feeling that most of us experience at one point or another. In many ways, envy is a "stealth sin," as it operates guilefully and often triggers feelings of shame. Unfortunately, envy was heightened during pandemic times. In particular, two major forms of envy made their appearance. First, there was the *quarantine* envy. Covid-19 brought wealth inequality even more into the open. Most probably, people and families who were stuck in small apartments were envious of those who during the quarantine had moved to their lavish country estates. And to add to these feelings of envy, some people would also be experiencing feelings of unfairness toward the places that had been in more advanced stages of reopening. A second form is *vaccine* envy. As the pandemic continued to surge, there have been great feelings of envy about vaccine abundance in the richer countries. Many people had been decrying the vaccine glut in a few nations and the relative drought almost everywhere else. Additionally, many high-income countries had locked up most of their near-term supply of the vaccines. As a caveat, however, I should add that despite envy's negative connotations, it can be helpful in regulating inequalities that have grown too widely. Thus, the surfacing of envy—hence the awareness of inequality—had led to a rethinking of the intellectual property and trademark laws that had been governing vaccine manufacturing.

Finally, there is pride, thought to be the source of all the other sins. This sin can manifest itself in many shapes and forms. Pride is rooted in self-centeredness and the need to put our own desires, urges, wants, and whims before the welfare of other people. No wonder that pride has always been perceived as being the most difficult sin to be rooted out, as it is the most hidden, secret, and deceitful of all vices. And the pandemic demonstrated how this sin became magnified in the context of leadership. Many leaders, when put in a position of power, seemed to become irrationally self-confident about their abilities, increasingly reluctant to listen to the advice of others, and progressively more impulsive in their actions. Therefore, it would not come as a surprise that the speed and scope of the pandemic posed extraordinary challenges for leaders. Many of them proved to be arrogant and highly incompetent. At great cost to human life, some even ignored the pandemic or downplayed the threat of Covid-19, thus delaying taking any form of action. Tragically, this hubris, and refusal to accept that they were wrong, has led to a loss of life on a massive scale. Several of these more prideful leaders also took advantage of the pandemic by invoking their inner autocrat. For them, the restrictive measures that had to be imposed were used as an opportunity to dent democratic norms and to seize more power. However, the important question raised was whether they would be willing to give up their near-total authority once the crisis associated with the pandemic had passed. Many of them came to realize that it is far easier to govern by decree than to govern within limits. And prideful leaders are very good at taking power but not very good at handing it back.

Post Pandemic Leadership Virtues

The exploration of the seven deadly sins during the Covid-19 pandemic can also reveal what virtuous behavior should look like.

The pandemic has brought our vices to the fore but also given us a chance to rethink what business leadership should look like now and for the foreseeable future. As I mentioned before, during the pandemic, many leaders refused to acknowledge their own limits, faults, or wrongdoings, raising questions about whether their hyper-masculine leadership style is still appropriate. Prideful as many of them turned out to be, a great number of them have not lived up to the challenge.

In comparison, the leadership style of female leaders—which tend to be more relational, empathetic, inclusive, and socially oriented—became an important factor in promoting the legitimacy of and the compliance with the lockdown measures, while also offering affective support and a longer-term vision on how to overcome the crisis. Clearly, they seemed to be much better equipped to deal with the invisible enemy called Covid-19. Thus, it could very well be that because of the pandemic and other natural calamities like climate change, we need to change our perceptions of what effective leadership should look like in the future.

Perhaps, in searching for the most effective leadership style in this day-and-age, we would do well to direct our focus not on the seven cardinal sins, but rather on the seven virtues. These virtues were originally presented by the poet Aurelius Clemens Prudentius in his poem *Psychomachia* in the early fifth century. In this work, *chastity* or self-control would overcome lust by controlling passion, leveraging this energy toward the good of others. There is also *temperance* which would cure gluttony by implanting the desire to be healthy. In addition, in the poem, *charity* tempered greed by putting the desire to help others above our own needs. Furthermore, *patience* would disarm wrath by allowing time to understand the needs and desires of others before acting. And *diligence* would be the counterpoint to slothfulness by placing the best interest of other people above a life of ease and relaxation. In addition, *kindness* would prevent envy by placing the desire to help others above one's own needs. Finally, there's *humility*, which would cure pride by removing boastfulness through an attitude of service.

Of course, the seven deadly sins will always be part of our true nature. All of us possess a modicum of lust, gluttony, greed, hate, sloth, envy, and pride. Like it or not, these seven deadly sins will always be with us. In fact, life would be quite tedious without them. Our challenge will be, however, to exert a degree of control over these so-called vices. If not, as the pandemic has shown dramatically, the results can be disastrous.

3

Evil: Reality and Imagination

> *The opportunity for doing mischief is found a hundred times a day, and of doing good once in a year.*
> —*Voltaire*
>
> *The evil that is in the world almost always comes of ignorance, and good intentions may do as much harm as malevolence if they lack understanding.*
> —*Albert Camus*

While the Covid-19 pandemic could be viewed as a freak accident, what could be said about a more deliberate evil—something that isn't due to circumstances beyond our control? For example, what do you imagine the people who have been working at Evil Corp, a group of Russian cybercriminals, might be like? Does the name of their organization indicate the kinds of individuals it attracts? Is what they do evil—and can they then be called evil? The people who have been working for Evil Corp have very successfully targeted some of the world's most well-protected corporations. They have stolen their credentials. They have crippled their IT infrastructure by encrypting their computers and servers. And their evildoing has enabled them to demand multimillion dollar ransoms. In fact, the decade-long worldwide cybercrime, ransomware spree by its alleged leader, Maksim Yakubets, has been responsible for losses amounting to hundreds of millions of dollars.

But belonging to such an organization must have a certain appeal. Evil has always stimulated the human imagination. After all, we are fascinated by real-life dark "heroes" like Bernie Madoff, the instigator of the largest Ponzi scheme in history, and Jordan Belfort, the Wolf of Wall Street, as well as the villains of fairy tales and films. "Crime" is the largest and most successful genre of popular fiction. Could our interest have something to do with a need to better understand evil, to know where evil people could be hiding, and how they differ from you and me?

Of course, recognizing evil is important: villains don't helpfully enter the world equipped with horns and cloven feet, giving off a foul stench. The power of evil is that it isn't always easy to spot. But recognizing evil could be a lifesaver, while failing to recognize a potentially dangerous person or situation could be fatal.

So, how do we begin to recognize evil? Generally speaking, evil involves human destructiveness, people who take pleasure in intentionally hurting others and behaving in ways that harm, abuse, demean, dehumanize, or destroy the innocent.

Why do people behave like this? What makes them do terrible things? Taking a deep dive in search of explanations, we find that evil acts are often used as a means to an end, for example, to gain wealth, sex, status, or power. There are also situations where evil is a response to threats to the self. Some people are motivated to do evil to gain self-esteem, to live up to a grandiose self-image. In these situations, vindictive acts can be weapons used to put other people down. However, many evil acts are the result of idealistic fanaticism. As the French philosopher Blaise Pascal put it, "Men never do evil so completely and cheerfully as when they do it from religious conviction." Far too often, people who live according to an ideology are convinced that there's only one truth, and this belief, of being in possession of a special truth, lies at the root of much of the world's evil. Moreover, there are some people who engage in evil acts because of social and ideological pressures to conform, willingly following the orders of others.

Evil people even create so-called evil enterprises. For example, many organizations subscribe to corrupt practices, including polluting the environment, manufacturing and marketing unsafe products, corporate bribery, and encouraging their employees to engage in corporate violence. Within these kinds of organizations, we can usually find a dominant coalition that has played a leading role in the enacted evil. Either directly or through the people who work for them, these organizational leaders engage in corrupt practices that benefit themselves and other stakeholders.

The Ambiguity of Evil

As evil sits on the spectrum of right or wrong, how do we decide what's what? How do we determine what constitutes a truly evil act? After all, life isn't one-dimensional. People aren't simply divided into camps of good and evil. Evil is a highly ambiguous concept. Criminals can have their virtues just as honest people can have a darker side. What's seen as an evil act by one person, could be considered quite differently by another. Good and evil aren't fixed, stable qualities. Instead, they are constantly trading places. For some, suicide bombers are princes of darkness; to others, they are heroic freedom fighters. The truth is that there is good and bad in every individual, in every nation, in every racial group, and in every religion. Even the vilest of people can do good from time to time. In fact, it's a rare individual who is completely evil.

However, this doesn't mean that we shouldn't bother to learn more about evil. After all, if we don't acknowledge it, it might capture us. We need to understand the moral significance of atrocities like torture, sexual abuse, mass shootings, psychopathic serial killing, mob violence, terrorist attacks, and genocide. Only by obtaining greater clarity about the nature and origin of evil can we hope to prevent such things from happening repeatedly.

A promising beginning to understanding evil is to take a hard look at ourselves. The Russian writer Aleksander Solzhenitsyn once said, "The battleline between good and evil runs through the heart of every man." Most of us have at some time found ourselves struggling with evil thoughts. We may have felt the wish to do something unpleasant, to give someone their just deserts. But do these desires mean that we are evil—that we have a darker side? The Swiss psychiatrist/psychoanalyst Carl Jung thought so. He imagined that each of us has an aspect within our personality that we choose to reject and repress—a part of ourselves that we don't like or think society would find unacceptable. According to Jung, we prefer to push this "beast within" into our unconscious. But again, does this mean that we are evil? After all, thoughts are very different from actions. Evil thoughts remain just that unless we feel compelled to act on them.

The question of whether evil is a characteristic that lies dormant in all of us received renewed attention in response to the atrocities committed by Nazi fanatics during World War II. In those dark years, the forces of evil came to the fore in ways that were far beyond most people's darkest imaginings. Sadly, the Holocaust of World War II is only one example of humanity's capacity for cruelty toward our own kind. Looking at the history of humankind, we can see that the forces of evil have triumphed more often than we would like to admit. Evildoers have always been with us. Atrocities have always been part of the human condition. Consequently, given the human potential to do evil, it shouldn't come as a surprise that many moral, political, and legal philosophers have been preoccupied with this question. How was it possible for the Holocaust to happen? Was there something evil within the perpetrators or were the evildoers themselves the victims of circumstance?

Obedience to Authority

The philosopher and political theorist Hannah Arendt, who witnessed the trial of the war criminal Adolf Eichmann in Jerusalem in 1961, noted that Eichmann could have been merely an administrator following orders.[1] She introduced the term "the banality of evil" to imply that evil acts are not necessarily committed by evil people. Instead, she suggested that Eichmann could have been, to all appearances, a rather ordinary, "normal" bureaucrat. However, her statement also implied that if

---

[1] Hannah Arendt (2006). *Eichmann in Jerusalem*. London: Penguin.

unexceptional, supposedly normal people are capable of evil, then the atrocities perpetrated during the Holocaust and other genocides could be easily repeated, the recent war crimes that have been taking place in the Ukraine being an extremely disturbing example.

But was Arendt correct in making this observation? Were people like Eichmann just a dime a dozen? Was he merely representative of the population at large? Is there truth in her observation that evil starts when unremarkable people embark on seemingly unremarkable acts? And could it even be true that the most dangerous people in the world are not the tiny minority who instigate evil acts, but those who carry out these acts for them? Could it be that much of the evil in this world is caused by people blindly following orders, while others, knowing that what was being done was wrong, did nothing to stop it?

Arendt questioned the notion of obedience to authority to explain why quite ordinary people were able to do incredibly evil things. Could it be true that the guards in the extermination camps, who were otherwise seemingly normal, family-loving men, were simply following orders? Could that explain why they willingly ran these camps like manufacturing plants, obediently delivering to the crematoria their daily quota of murdered bodies? Were these people just like you and me?

Many of us have found ourselves in situations when we should have taken a stand but to our utter disgrace have remained silent bystanders. There is some truth in the observation that non-action is the devil's most powerful weapon: the devil can't always convince a good person to do wrong but can keep someone from doing what's right. Evil triumphs when good people do nothing. In the vacuum created by fear, ignorance, hunger, and want, it's evil, not good, that rushes in to fill the void. As Albert Einstein once said, "The world is a dangerous place to live, not because of the people who are evil, but because of the people who don't do anything about it." The sad truth is that some people engage in evil acts, while others see evil acts being done but don't attempt to stop it. The Holocaust survivor and Nobel laureate Elie Wiesel once said, "Indifference, to me, is the epitome of evil." Evil tends to rise to the surface when good people don't act. The impact of dysfunctional group dynamics can be devastating.

Group Dynamics

When I was thirteen, I engaged unwittingly (helped by my younger brother) in a small social science experiment. During the summer, our parents used to send the two of us to a youth camp for the whole, long school holiday. It made us old timers. We were the ones who knew how this summer camp functioned.

One summer we devised a practical joke that could be reframed as having an evil aspect. In hindsight, it is fair to say that we were budding social scientists, engaged in a human relations experiment. When the new cohort of kids arrived, we told them that it was a tradition in this camp that all newcomers had to participate in an initiation rite. We pointed to a bathtub filled with cold water, standing in the middle of the field. The idea was that each of them had to immerse him or herself in the tub. To our immense glee, thirty kids (all of them much bigger than us) lined up and submerged themselves, one after the other, in the ice-cold water. Our experiment was moving along seamlessly until misfortune struck in the form of the camp leader who passed by. Pretending to be outraged, he encouraged the newcomers to turn the tables on us. And we got our just desert, both ending up immersed in the tub.

Several years after our own experiment in obedience to authority, two social psychologists, Stanley Milgram and Philip Zimbardo, wanted to test whether it was true that ordinary people were capable of doing evil things when ordered to do so by individuals in a position of authority.[2] Obviously, their motivation for embarking on such an experiment was to find answers to the question of how the Nazis were able to induce people to commit atrocities—why seemingly normal people turned to evil in circumstances that required their obedience or allowed them to do evil with no consequences.

Milgram's experiment tested whether volunteers would give potentially lethal electric shocks to people when ordered to do so by an

---

[2] Stanley Milgram (1963). Behavioral Study of Obedience, *Journal of Abnormal and Social Psychology*. 67 (4), 371–378: Philip Zimbardo (1972). *The Stanford Prison Experiment: A Simulation Study of the Psychology of Imprisonment Conducted August 1971 at Stanford University*. Stanford: Stanford University; Philip Zimbardo (2008). *The Lucifer Effect: Understanding How Good People Turn Evil*. New York: Random House.

authority figure. The shocking outcome was that the participants were quite willing to do so. In Zimbardo's study, a mock prison experiment, the students who took on the role of "guards" abused the assigned "prisoners" with impunity. The dramatic results of these two studies revealed how quickly ordinary people were prepared to engage in extraordinary evil acts when placed in a toxic environment. The extremely troublesome conclusion to be drawn from these studies was that under the right circumstances all of us could be capable of resorting to evil acts. To quote Zimbardo, "The line between good and evil is permeable and almost anyone can be induced to cross it if pressured by situational forces."

The Milgram and Zimbardo experiments showed that people in positions of authority could easily sway people in subordinate positions to do unimaginable things. Unfortunately, in today's world the truth of this is out there for us all to see. We are frequently appalled by the consequences of toxic leadership. Too many leaders know how to manipulate their followers into engaging in horrendous activities. Some people have a desire to control others, encourage their dependency needs, and discourage their capacity to think for themselves. In pursuit of their own selfish motives, they can push their followers to engage in evil acts.

Subsequent research, however, has shown that the Milgram and Zimbardo studies failed to provide evidence for the hypothesis that *all of us* turn to evil when placed in certain situations. In fact, during both experiments, numerous people refused to follow orders. The reactions of these people point out the significance of free will. They denote that we do have a choice, that we can use our free will to choose between good and evil, that we don't need to be pawns in others' games. But will we be capable of acting with discernment when faced with suspect, authoritative directions? Will we be able to exert a degree of self-control?

In many instances, evil behavior is also a consequence of a loss of control. For example, evil acts are often committed under the influence of drugs or alcohol. In the heat of passion, the moral enormity of evil actions often gets lost. And, of course, there is also the question of personality. People who assault, rape, and murder may lack sufficient impulse control.

The Dark Psyche

The question of impulse control points to the psyche of people who do evil. What kinds of personalities do they have? Why do some individuals take pleasure in evil acts? What motivates them to carry them out? Here, I'm considering a spectrum that ranges from less obvious personae, such as school bullies and ransomware trolls—even those otherwise upstanding members of society who see evil being done but remain bystanders—to the most malevolent evildoers, like rapists and serial killers.

Although the personalities of evil people come in various shades, several possess qualities that can be summarized as the "dark dyad," a toxic combination of narcissism (self-centeredness, a need for constant, excessive admiration, and a sense of entitlement) and psychopathy (manipulative, vindictive, with callous insensitivity to the feelings of others).[3] People with these characteristics are more likely to engage in evil actions.

Nurture and Nature

How do people become this way? Is it a function of nature or nurture? Is becoming an evildoer a developmental issue or are these people simply born bad?

From a nurture point of view, observing children with psychopathic tendencies, there seems to be a strong causal connection between a dysfunctional upbringing and deviant behavior. For some, exposure to abuse during childhood creates conditions that make it more likely that they will embrace evil. These are children who never developed the security that comes with feelings of self-confidence and personal competence. Due to their personal history, feelings of compassion and empathy are alien to them. Instead, the most significant themes in their life are anger, hatred, envy, and vindictiveness.

From the nature perspective, neuroscientists have investigated some of the biological mechanisms that could explain why certain people are

---

[3] It is not what some people call the "Dark Triad," a term that refers to a trio of negative personality characteristics: narcissism, psychopathy, and Machiavellianism. People who use the term triad, forget that behavior patterns such as narcissism and psychopathy are inclusive of Machiavellianism.

more violent than others. Most of the neurological research into psychopathology has focused on regions of the neocortex of the brain that govern impulse control. Some neuroscientists have suggested that a breakdown can occur in the feedback mechanisms between the amygdala and the higher, cognitive cortical structures of the brain, affecting the emotional pathways that regulate judgment and action. However, the application of neuroscience to the understanding of evil is still in its infancy.

Evolutionary psychologists have also added to the nature/nurture controversy. Advocates of the "selfish gene" theory have suggested that assault, rape, and murder could even be seen as rational acts, in that they could have been beneficial to our species' survival. Those of our paleolithic ancestors who were willing to participate in violent actions might have been the beneficiaries of more resources, and subsequently blessed with more descendants.

Taking these various perspectives into consideration, the origins of evil could be explained as the outcome of the mutual interplay of biological, psychological, and social factors. But whatever its origins, the essential question is how to prevent evil from coming to the fore.

Preventing Evil

Most of us look at genocide, suicide bombing, and similar acts of extreme violence as completely incomprehensible. However, it may be that the reason why we react in this way is because we don't really want to understand such atrocities. We prefer to keep such things beyond the common realm of human experience, rather than face up to the horrifying fact that people who seem just like us can decide to do evil and appear to obtain pleasure from it. However, if we do this, we give these people a power that they should never have. "See no evil, hear no evil, speak no evil" is no way to deal with the problem of why such horrendous things happen and how we should respond to them.

Mental Acrobatics

The human mind has an infinite capacity for rationalization and compartmentalization. Human reasoning can excuse any form of evildoing. We can find justifications for anything, from cheating in exams, to participating in crooked financial deals, to the senseless slaughter of thousands of people. And tragically, many of the people who feel justified in doing horrible things to others may even believe in the correctness of their actions. In fact, more evil is done in the name of righteousness than in any other name. What mental acrobatics do people like Bashar al-Assad, the president of Syria, Alexander Lukashenko, the leader of Belarus, or Min Aung Hlaing, the military dictator of Myanmar, perform to rationalize their atrocities? Can they sleep well at night? Do they experience any feelings of shame or guilt about what they have been doing? Sadly, many of the people who make wars, the people who kill and torture, imagine that they are virtuous, respectable people with noble ideals. All too often, they're able to construct their own convoluted narrative to explain and justify their evil actions. The paradoxical nature of what they say and what they do, however, escapes them.

Ironically, perpetrators of mass murder and torture may express love for their children—they may make touching comments about family life—while having no compassion at all for their victims. Instead, they have become masters of compartmentalization. They know how to mentally separate conflicting thoughts, emotions, or experiences to avoid the discomfort of contradiction. In fact, many who participate in horrific activities imagine that they're doing something great, and that their activities are morally justified. Unfortunately, they don't realize that the essence of morality is the ability to question the morality of what they're doing.

What Is Moral?

What constitutes morality has been the subject of great controversy. Is it possible to speak of morality in absolute terms, or is morality dependent on circumstances? Doesn't each society develop its own set of norms and standards for acceptable behavior, thus contributing to the notion that morality is entirely culturally conditioned?

If we assume that there is no such thing as morality in absolute terms, how can we deal with people who torture, murder, or engage in child abuse? Shouldn't they be called to account? Should we just let them be? Is it morally justifiable to hold on to the notion that morality is relative when evil acts are undeniably concrete? Isn't some form of judgment warranted, given the terrible consequences of these people's actions?

The atrocities of World War II and beyond emphasized that the ultimate struggle between good and evil takes place inside each of us. Each of us has a responsibility to make thoughtful, moral choices, and we abnegate that responsibility if we refuse to judge a challenging situation when faced with it; if we sit on the fence, neither agreeing nor disagreeing; if we hang onto the belief that there are no absolutes; and if we have no sense of personal responsibility for the actions we take. We need to accept that the responsibility for choosing between good and evil is within the reach of each of us.

The Greek physician Hippocrates realized this dilemma a long, long time ago. He believed that we need to live according to the principle of "*primum non nocere*," meaning "first, do no harm." This maxim—one of the principal precepts of bioethics taught worldwide to people in the helping professions—can be considered a basic guideline applying to all moral choices.

Given the human capacity to do evil to other human beings, we should never stop asking ourselves the question of whether what we're doing is good or evil—whether we're causing harm to others. Being prepared to pose this question is a responsibility we have toward ourselves. And it is an awesome responsibility that we should not relegate to other people. As Confucius said, "He who searches for evil must first look at his own reflection." We should never let our guard down in questioning that what we're doing is morally justified. Furthermore, we should constantly remind ourselves that nobody is immune to evil. We're all prone to regressive processes. It's very easy to enter the dark abyss where evil dwells. In fact, there are many regressive social and psychological forces at work that can easily lead us astray and can create a fertile basis for evil. This makes finding ways of prevention a real challenge.

Creating a Secure Base

Fyodor Dostoevsky wrote, "Nothing is easier than to denounce the evildoer; nothing is more difficult than to understand him." To prevent evil from coming to the fore, we need to make sense of its contributing factors. We need to know why some people do evil things. Also, we need to understand how evil imprisons people.

Although moral development is a life-long challenge, its foundations are created early in life.[4] From the earliest years, the challenge for caregivers is to help children feel secure in their skin—to imbue them with a solid sense of self-confidence. This is what child development is all about. Without having acquired a secure base, it will be difficult for children to face life's many challenges and deal with the inevitable setbacks that are part of the vicissitudes of life. Without a secure base, it will also be hard for a child to acquire a questioning mindset and to learn from experience.[5]

Children acquire an understanding of what's right and wrong in various ways. First, they learn by observing the behavior of the people who are most important to them, usually (it is to be hoped) their parents. Hence, to help them understand the differences between right and wrong, the challenge for parents is to create congruence between what they say and what they do. Consistency in the way they handle their children is of utmost importance.

Fortunately, with respect to moral development, Homo sapiens has a flying start. We possess a built-in capacity to respond to signals given by others. In fact, as social beings, humans are "programmed" to learn from one another. In human interaction, behavioral mimicry—the automatic imitation of gestures, postures, mannerisms, and other motor movements—is all-pervasive. And it is this human proclivity to mimicry that creates pro-social behavior. From our earliest beginnings, the ability to interconnect with each other—to understand each other's feelings—was a great advantage for our species' survival. It would have been very

---

[4] Jean Piaget (1997). *The Moral Judgement of the Child*. New York: Simon & Schuster; Lawrence Kohlberg (1981). *Essays on Moral Development, Vol. I: The Philosophy of Moral Development*. San Francisco: Harper & Row.
[5] John Bowlby (2005). *A Secure Base*. London: Routledge.

difficult for Homo sapiens to prosper without cooperative behavior. Neuroscientists have even hypothesized that the human brain even possesses mirror neurons, cells that become activated when they see someone else doing something.[6] It is thought that these mirror neurons allow human beings to literally feel what others feel—to "live" their emotions.

According to these neuroscientists, these mirror neurons are responsible for emotional contagion, that is, conscious and unconscious processes that trigger similar emotions and behavior patterns in other people.[7] This process of emotional contagion helps synchronize our emotions and enables us to express our wants and needs to others through body language, facial expressions, and emotional assertions. These mirror neurons determine empathic and social behavior, fundamental processes in fostering learning and development.

Thus, just as there are phases of physical and mental development, there are phases of moral development. Taking the mirroring process as a starting point, the internalization of what's right and wrong very much depends on what children experience in their home environment—the kind of "contagion" they're exposed to while growing up. Children come to realize that certain types of behavior will be rewarded, while others will meet with disapproval. If there is "good-enough" parenting, the focus will be on reinforcing positive behavior rather than punishing what's perceived as negative. Children learn how *not* to get into trouble. They internalize correct and incorrect behavior.

Depending on the parents' consistency in applying the rules, children will also learn to assess whether these rules are fair or not. And if the parents have provided a sufficiently secure base, children will become courageous enough to challenge these rules in situations when they believe that they're not applied correctly. They want to ensure that everyone affected by these rules is treated fairly. Step by step, during these negotiations of what's believed to be fair, children acquire a deeper understanding of the difference between "good" and "bad" behavior, an understanding that will provide the foundation for more intricate moral thinking in the

---

[6] Giacomo Rizzolatti and Laila Craighero (2004). The mirror-neuron system, *Annual Review of Neuroscience*, 27, 169–192, DOI: https://doi.org/10.1146/annurev.neuro.27.070203.144230
[7] Manfred F. R. Kets de Vries (2022). *The Daily Perils of Executive Life: How to Survive When Dancing on Quicksand*. London: Palgrave.

future. And as moral development progresses, reactions of shame and guilt come to the fore in situations where children know that they have broken the rules.

Although parent–child interactions are significant in creating an understanding of what moral behavior is all about, children become even more practiced in making "correct" moral choices during interactions that take place within a larger social context. They will encounter children who behave in selfish, destructive, or mean ways, and have to deal with them. When this happens, they may experience feelings of anger, hatred, envy, or resentment. If they believe that they have been wronged, children may have the knee-jerk reaction of wanting to retaliate. On these kinds of occasions "good enough" parenting will come into play. When unpleasant incidents occur, the parents' response to the child's emotions is critical. Their challenge is to "hold" their children—to put them at ease and prevent them from acting in a similar way. These kinds of incidents give parents the opportunity to teach their children the wisdom of taking time out in order to cool down. It enables them to explain that there are more constructive ways of dealing with frustration.

Gradually, if parents have created a positive learning environment, children will be able to process these situations by themselves. They come to appreciate that there are positive ways of managing their emotional repertoire. They learn to go beyond knee-jerk reactions and to understand why certain people behave the way they do.

Eventually, children learn to recognize when they might become upset before they actually do so. They learn to manage strong emotional reactions, to take a deep breath, and regroup. Consciously and unconsciously, they have metabolized their destructive impulses and understood the power of introspection and self-awareness. The ability to engage in this psychological "work" is part of their emotional and social "armor," helping them to determine what would be the "right" or "wrong" action to take.

If there has been good enough parenting, and good enough moral development, children will know when something isn't right and will have the courage to say so.[8] Although there will always be powerful socio-

---

[8] Donald W. Winnicott (1973). *The Child, the Family, and the Outside World*. London: Penguin.

psychological forces at play that could encourage obedience to authority, children will be aware that there's also such a thing as personal responsibility.

Difficult experiences can be teaching opportunities for parents to explain their intentions to their children and help them channel their destructive responses toward more creative endeavors, including "good works," even if only on a small scale. Challenging encounters give parents the chance to teach their children that goodness is its own reward and that helping others can enrich their own appreciation of life. And if parents successfully create such a positive educational trajectory for their children, it will act as a bulwark against evil. The kind of moral education that emphasizes personal responsibility is an antidote to ignorance.

Human behavior will always be the product of the forces of nature and nurture. But, as I have suggested, various psychological and socio-cultural factors will determine how these innate biological processes play themselves out. Within this matrix of human nature, depending on childhood experiences, specific behavioral patterns will come to the fore. These will determine the extent to which competitive and cooperative behavior will evolve, the balance between aggressive and helpful behavior, and whether compassion and empathy will become an essential part of a person's character.

Thus, from a developmental point of view, humanity's most important challenge is how to raise non-violent children. And even though children may start with small acts of kindness, it is through such acts that we can prepare the way for a better world. Starting in a small way, each new generation can have a positive influence on institutions, communities, and societies. Conversely, neglected, or misdirected children, starting in equally small ways, can leave small marks of unpleasantness and, as adults, their behavior can negatively affect humankind. We only need to think of the abusive childhoods of Hitler and Stalin to see how this has played out in our recent past.

Even if there should turn out to be such a thing as a psychopathy gene, we could expect its effects to be ameliorated through positive, nurturing childrearing practices. Biology isn't necessarily destiny. The children of evil people don't have to be evil. They can turn into good people. Therefore, it is a social imperative to make an all-out effort to prevent the abuse and emotional neglect of children and to create an ambiance characterized by responsive affection and nurture, non-punitive guidance, and value-based learning experiences. With "good-enough" parenting, children will become compassionate, empathic, altruistic, courageous, and less susceptible to outbursts of anger. They will have a greater ability to understand the feelings of others and appreciate the benefits of healing, reconciliation, and forgiveness.

Don't Be a Bystander

Every time we are faced with moral dilemmas, we should remind ourselves that the most common defense put forward by evildoers is that they didn't know what was happening. And even if they knew, they may claim that they weren't responsible for their actions; they were just following orders. These are unacceptable excuses. People like Eichmann were not just helpless puppets within the Nazi hierarchy. They accepted the dehumanization of others. They willingly corrupted themselves, starting with small transgressions. And as they began to sell their soul in small quantities—making a trivial compromise here, rationalizing a minor evil there—eventually real evil dropped its disguise and bit them in the face.

We all have an obligation to refuse to let the bad win. We should never let evil hold the field. If we fail to stop evildoers, we are not only protecting them but also becoming willing enablers. We cannot be bystanders. Good intentions can sometimes do as much harm as malevolence. Often, the terrible things that happen in our world are not down to the people who do evil, but to basically decent people who refuse to confront the existence of evil. If we are not courageous enough to take a stand against evil, there is no hope for humanity.

Societal Considerations

As Carl Jung pointed out, one of the biggest difficulties in contemporary society is that we try to locate the evil in other people rather than take personal responsibility for it. Too often, we project onto others what we fear within ourselves, and those others become the recipients of our hatred. When we feel wronged, we split people into camps of good and bad, often encouraged by the behavior of populist, demagogue-like leaders. Unfortunately, when we fail to look within ourselves, we fail to see the extent to which we harbor moral ambiguities. Each of us has a personal responsibility for the moral choices we make because individual behavior creates the foundation for group, community, institutional, and governmental behavior.

Taking business organizations as examples, business leaders shouldn't have to make a choice between profitability and social responsibility. They need to recognize "the tragedy of the commons." Too many people act independently based on their own self-interest and contrary to the common good. They endanger the world through their uncoordinated actions. A much more constructive way for business leaders to act is to have a shared sense of doing good. They need to connect what they do with a purpose beyond profit. In other words, in organizational life, they need to create situations of profit with purpose. Given the fragility of our planet, organizational leaders should make social responsibility part of their mandate.

The same can be said of other institutions, including governments. Can it be morally right for governments to do things that individuals aren't permitted to do? Isn't it the function of a well-functioning government to make it easy for people to do good and very difficult for them to do evil? Making this happen, however, will very much depend on its leadership.

Unfortunately, many of our political leaders are responsible for much of the evil present in our world. And given the scale on which they operate, the evil they create can have exponentially negative effects. Far too easily, demagogue-like leaders (helped by the social media that have become a new weapon of mass destruction) can reframe evil into something that is presented as heroic. Once in public life, evil is easily perpetuated. In comparison, actions for the general good are rare, extremely fragile, and difficult to disseminate.

Clearly, instead of being led by populist, demagogue-like leaders, we need value-driven, non-divisive leaders who aren't motivated by the politics of hatred—leaders who encourage independent thinking, aren't obsessed by control, and don't abuse their power to dominate other people. Given the corruptive influence of power, however, this will be a real balancing act. And as the obedience to authority studies have shown, when decent people are placed in evil situations—and in spite of their basic decency—the outcome can still be horrendous. The danger that people will lose their ability to think for themselves is ever-present. This is why it is imperative that there are countervailing powers within governments made of strong civil institutions, including an independent judiciary, and an independent press.

Avoiding the Darkness

Much evil starts when we begin to treat people as things, when our caring side is muted, and when there is a lack of compassion and empathy. All evil begins with the belief that the existence of other people is far less precious than our own. It is a sad truth that when we stop acknowledging the humanity of others—when we perceive others as sub-human and to blame for everything that is wrong in the world—we see evil emerging.

Fortunately, as part of our developmental trajectory, most human beings possess the qualities of compassion and empathy. And these characteristics can be extremely powerful forces, so much so that they can serve as an antidote to evil. When we respond to other people's needs, when we engage in selfless acts, we make ourselves and others feel better. In fact, the people who feel best about themselves are those who do the most for others. And although, at times, group dynamic processes may exploit our worst instincts, these socio-psychological forces can also be called upon to cultivate the best in us. Like evil, altruism is also readily responsive to situational forces.

When we look around, we can see that many people, at great cost to themselves, carry out acts of kindness, both big and small, and that doing so seems to put them in a zone of transcendence. They have come to realize that doing good induces others to reciprocate—that doing good can be contagious. Even though nobody can save the world, each of us can do a little bit of good while we live our lives. We aren't helpless puppets controlled by the forces of evil. We don't have to go into that darkness.

Mahatma Gandhi once said, "When I despair, I remember that all through history the way of truth and love have always won. There have been tyrants and murderers, and for a time, they can seem invincible, but in the end, they always fall. Think of it—always."

The challenge for each of us is to learn to tame our private demons and conquer evil wherever it looks us in the face. In other words, being good is something we must choose over and over again, all day, every day, for the rest of our lives. Each moment of our lives, each decision we take, gives us the choice of working toward the light or sinking into the darkness. Every day, we have the opportunity to do good and to be good. Every day, we can be kind to others. So why not take advantage of it? Even though we may do good without receiving any acknowledgment, we should never feel disheartened. At least, we have tried to make the world a better place, however small our good action might be. If we spread goodness, it will continue to be spread by our descendants, a wonderful legacy to leave behind. The happiest among us are not those who get more, but those who give more.

4

The Psychology of White-Collar Criminals

> We hang the petty thieves and appoint the great ones to public office.
> —Aesop
>
> It is criminal to steal a purse, daring to steal a fortune, a mark of greatness to steal a crown. The blame diminishes as the guilt increases.
> —Friedrich Schiller

Introduction

Some time ago, I was reading in the *Financial Times* the account of Australian financier Lex Greensill and his partner-in-crime, the Indian-born British businessman Sanjeev Gupta. At the time of my reading, Greensill, the founder of Greensill Capital, had not only filed for insolvency protection, but was also facing legal scrutiny over alleged fraudulent activities. Also being called into question was his relationship with Sanjeev Gupta, whose financial wizardry was being scrutinized by the authorities. The latter had been described as "a scrappy outsider on a mission to rescue dying industrial communities," earning him the nickname of "savior of steel." Like Greensill Capital, the viability of Gupta's extremely opaque empire had been questioned. Yet none of this seemed to deter the two gentlemen from continuing to live an indulgent, lavish lifestyle, with estates, private airplanes, and luxury yachts. In 2020, even as the financial foundations of his empire were falling apart, Gupta bought a six-story mansion in London's upmarket Belgravia for £42 million—albeit in his wife's name.

Reading the account of these people in the *Financial Times*, I was reminded of *The Wizard of Lies,* an American TV biopic of Bernie Madoff whose Wall Street company was one of the world's largest investment funds. Madoff enjoyed a stellar reputation as a successful and influential financier, broker, financial consultant, and generous philanthropist. Eventually, however, the house of cards he had built fell apart. It turned out that his success as an investor was a sham. In truth, Madoff had built a Ponzi scheme that robbed $65 billion from his unsuspecting victims, making it the largest fraud case in US history. When reality hit, Madoff was sentenced to 150 years in prison. And if that judgment wasn't devastating enough, his gigantic fraud had horrific consequences for his family.

The term "white-collar crime" has been associated with the educated and affluent ever since it was first coined by criminologist Edwin Sutherland in 1939. Sutherland defined it as "a crime committed by a person of respectability and high social status in the course of his occupation."[1] White-collar crimes tend to refer to financially motivated, nonviolent crimes that generally take place in the office environment and involve the manipulation of accounting and finance systems. Typical white-collar crimes include Ponzi schemes, insider trading, fraud, bribery, forgery, money-laundering, embezzlement, cybercrime, identity theft, and copyright infringement. Sutherland also pointed out that, taking a socio-demographical point of view, white-collar criminals are quite different from the typical street criminal, in that they are married, have an above-average education and a high income, are regularly employed, are homeowners, and have moderate to strong ties to their community, family, and/or religion. To all appearances, they have no reason to commit a crime, but they still do. When their crime is detected, a common

---

[1] Edwin Sutherland (1949). *White Collar Crime*. New York: The Dryden Press, p. 272.

reaction is genuine incredulity, such is the faith of others in their integrity and the perceived unlikelihood that they would ever commit such an offense.

However, it is clear to see that white-collar crime is a serious problem. It is estimated that these high-level frauds cost the global economy over US$5 trillion every year.[2] Furthermore, from the point of view of the general public, white-collar crime appears to be a key reason why the approval and trust of businesspeople have eroded. According to Gallup's annual updates, business executives rank near the bottom on a list of professions in a category of perceived ethics and honesty.[3]

Financial costs aside, white-collar crimes often prove to be literally deadly. Consider, for instance, the 1984 Bhopal disaster in India, when a massive gas leak in a pesticide plant contributed to some 8000 deaths and half a million injuries. Or take the Chinese milk scandal of 2008, when it was discovered that top managers of the dairy company Sanlu were fully aware that a toxic compound used in making plastics was being added to its milk products. The contamination led to the poisoning of 300,000 people, mostly infants. Again, the recession of 2008 was a result of the manipulation of the real estate market by Wall Street firms, costing numerous Americans their homes and their savings. While the crude fraud schemes of a few people on Wall Street enabled them to build lavish beach houses in the Hamptons, other people's retirement funds were decimated, causing property values in their neighborhoods to collapse, and forcing over four million people into foreclosure. Another more recent example of fraud is the so-called diesel dupe. In 2015, car manufacturer Volkswagen was found to have inserted software in 11 million cars that would detect when they were being tested, changing their engine performance to improve their emission test results.

Why did these apparently respectable people and organizations do these awful things? What drove them? Did the environment in which they operated make them do it or were they deeply flawed from the start?

---

[2] https://www.crowe.com/global/news/fraud-costs-the-global-economy-over-us$5-trillion
[3] https://news.gallup.com/opinion/gallup/211793/ceos-employees-trust.aspx

The Fraud Triangle

To help us understand such behavior, we can apply the "Fraud Triangle," a conceptual framework commonly used in auditing to help explain the reasoning behind an individual's decision to commit fraud.[4] According to this framework, three major forces are at work: pressure, opportunity, and rationalization.

If we take *pressure*, the question becomes whether a company has strict parameters in place so that people are deterred from committing a crime, even if they want to do so. However, it may well be that these people operate in an ethically challenging environment, where a certain amount of deviant behavior is accepted—a culture of "let's see what we can get away with." In other words, will a person's propensity to become a white-collar criminal depend on how much they associate with other criminals? In a company where unethical and unlawful business practices are par for the course, those practices could become a form of learned behavior. For example, a company might pressure employees to participate in a crime, under the guise of incentivization, by offering a reward or compensation. If employees believe that they are being ordered to do something wrong, they might not have a sense of personal responsibility. They might think that "others" are responsible.

In fact, the specifics of a situation can play a significant role in determining people's behavior. *Opportunity* is essentially a situation or combination of circumstances that create a pathway toward fraud. For example, opportunities might be embedded in defective internal controls, inadequate accounting systems, a toxic, unethical corporate culture, or dysfunctional leadership. In addition, opportunity could be enlarged by perpetrators in positions of authority.

Again, if an enterprise is focused exclusively on profits, white-collar criminals may be able to *rationalize* that whatever they're doing is for the good of the organization. They could use the rallying cry, "Everybody does it." Another form of rationalization is to represent unethical practices as victimless crimes. For example, ethically challenged stockbrokers

---

[4] Donald R. Cressey (1972). *Other People's Money: Study in the Social Psychology of Embezzlement.* Belmont, California: Wadsworth Publishing Company.

may view what they are doing as harmless, as there are no direct victims of their actions. The same point can be made concerning inflated claims against insurance companies.

In fact, fraudsters are masters of rationalization, capable of compartmentalizing their feelings and personal ethics, denying responsibility, and absolving themselves from guilt. Extraordinarily, many of them are just as surprised at their egregious behavior as anyone else once the game is up. Whereas in an assault, rape, or robbery, an individual comes face-to-face with a victim, white-collar crimes tend to be more faceless. Quite often, perpetrators never actually interact with, see, or meet the people affected by their unethical practices. They may even go as far as to maintain that the victims had it coming to them, or that the system, the prosecution, the judge, the press, or anyone who condemns them for their actions is to blame. And if that doesn't do the job, another justification could be that they operate according to a superior set of laws or code of conduct. An example would be engaging in criminal activities in the name of their religious beliefs.

Studying the evolution of the behavior of people involved in white-collar crimes reveals that it tends to manifest itself first in small ways, so small that it may not even look like a fraud. Unfortunately, it generally continues to grow until it comes to bite them. In other words, most of corporate crooks aren't masterminds who carefully calculate their illegal acts, weighing the risks and rewards before embarking on their nefarious activities. In fact, more often than not, they haven't even thought through the consequences of their actions—the tragic story of Madoff being an excellent example of this. Instead, most people reach their decision to commit crime with very little thought or reflection. They never stop to consider that their actions will harm, even devastate, real people.

Many white-collar criminals never need to get close—physically or psychologically—to their victims. In fact, manipulative corporate conduct lacks the degree of intimacy that comes with, say, directly robbing someone. And proximity tends to affect how we assess a situation. With less proximity, the ability to empathize with the potential victims shrinks. Somehow, it creates a degree of detachment, and is hence the reason why many of these white-collar criminals fail to see the harm created by fraud, embezzlement, or price-fixing. Still, this begs the question whether a certain kind of person will be psychologically more predisposed to commit white-collar crime—even without pressure. And this question brings us to the people equation.

The People Equation

To expand the "Fraud Triangle," the idea of the "Fraud Diamond" has been introduced, adding a fourth model component: capability.[5] Fraud examiners have begun to recognize that a combination of personality and circumstances—a delicate "dance" between situational forces and personality dynamics—could help explain why people like Madoff, end up as white-collar criminals.

The Greed Factor

There is a social aspect connected to white-collar crime. From time immemorial, success in life has always been measured by the accumulation of possessions (tools, shelter, an abundance of food and other necessities, and any ancillary items that mark people as successful). Throughout history, these benchmarks of success have remained unchanged. In other words, as a marker of success, many people engage in conspicuous consumption—the practice of publicly displaying wealth rather than merely supplying our basic needs. Some people, however, experience a greater need to parade material objects as indicators of social position, power, and status. But while acquiring new "toys" or "trinkets" can provide a temporary high, all too soon these people adjust to their new possessions and, in terms of happiness, are back where they started. It is like they are on a hedonic treadmill, having to work harder and harder to earn more to buy, more to maintain the same level of satisfaction. Therefore, considering the greed factor, some people decide to look for short-cuts to maintain their level of satisfaction. Given their extravagant needs, their income is no longer sufficient. As a matter of fact, many white-collar criminals

---

[5] https://digitalcommons.kennesaw.edu/cgi/viewcontent.cgi?referer=https://www.google.com/&httpsredir=1&article=2546&context=facpubs

seem to be living way beyond their means at the time of their fraudulent activities, a factor that encourages them to do what they do. So, an attachment to hedonistic behavior, combined with opportune circumstances, can motivate and entice people toward unethical conduct.

Low Behavioral Self-Control

When some people are exposed to enough pressure and opportunity, a characteristic like low self-control can facilitate white-collar crime. Of course, exposure to stress can also affect people's self-control and inhibit restraint. If so, it can make some people more prone to lie and to cheat, at least temporarily. In other words, situational forces can affect innate factors, leading to criminal behavior. Generally speaking, however, it is executives with impaired self-control, thrill-seekers who look for instant gratification, who are more likely to resort to risky or reckless behavior and engage in white-collar crime.[6] For people with low self-control, risk-taking can turn into a drug. But like any drug, the effect of a hit soon wears off, so they engage in ever riskier behaviors to get the same high—until they self-destruct.

Narcissistic Disposition

White-collar criminals can get so caught up in the fact of how easy it is to transgress that they don't think about what might happen if they get caught. The reason they think this way may be related to a narcissistic disposition. Narcissistic individuals are only concerned with what is good for them, what will benefit them, or what will enhance their position. Generally speaking, true narcissists have illusions of grandeur and possibly exhibitionistic tendencies. They are always on the lookout for uncritical admiration. But their inflated sense of self often hides unexpressed feelings of inadequacy and inferiority. This explains why they're always looking for constant positive reinforcement from others, at every level of

---

[6] https://knowledge.insead.edu/blog/insead-blog/managing-thrill-seekers-4793

life. Narcissists also possess feelings of entitlement. They believe that the rules apply to everyone else—but not to them. And their superior attitude toward others makes them quite convincing, even when they're engaged in fraudulent activities. In fact, because narcissists think that everyone around them is beneath them—and less smart than they are—they are led to the false belief that no one is smart enough to catch them if they engage in crime.

Corporate Psychopathy

There is also the aspect of psychopathy or antisocial behavior. Clinical psychopathy is characterized by four features: callous affect, interpersonal manipulation, erratic lifestyle, and antisocial behavior.[7] However, in the context of corporate psychopathy, there is also an absence of empathy, guilt, and remorse when people exploit others for their highly personal ends. Basically, corporate psychopaths lack the ability to appreciate the emotional impact of their actions on others. Like true psychopaths, they are less likely to feel the same natural tendencies of guilt or remorse that ought to accompany their wrongdoings. However, people with these antisocial (psychopathic) tendencies—these psychopaths "light"—typically appear quite normal. But the mask of normality hides people who are always on the lookout for opportunities to meet their deep-seated need for power, status, and money. They are masters at sizing up situations quickly and manipulating others to cooperate with their schemes. Sadly enough, their charm can keep their victims in the dark for quite some time. What's more, even when they are caught, their charm often helps them to talk their way out of the criminal activities in which they are engaged. Many successful fraudsters have the ability to lie convincingly and convince themselves of their lies. Not surprisingly, people with this kind of personality makeup are often quite successful in large organizations, which are great places for them to hide in. In reality, however, their apparent success flows all too often from a series of subversions, betrayals, and nonstop rule breaking. Corporate psychopaths in senior

---

[7] Manfred F. R. Kets de Vries (2014). The psycho-path to disaster: coping with SOB executives, *Organizational Dynamics*, 43 (1), 17–26.

positions, given their talent for persuading and manipulating others, can influence the moral climate of entire organizations—that is, alter the scope of what are perceived as acceptable norms and behaviors. This can in turn normalize the sorts of behaviors that can contribute to the institutionalization of acts of white-collar crime.

Neurocriminology

In the context of white-collar crime, criminologists have also resorted to neurological studies (similar to what has been mentioned in Chap. 3), particularly looking at the functioning of the amygdala, the part of the brain that drives the so-called fight or flight response and where empathy and emotions are processed. MRI scans have shown that psychopaths tend to have an undersized amygdala and significantly weaker connections between the region of the brain associated with evaluating rewards (the nucleus accumbens—the basal forebrain) and the region associated with decision-making (the ventromedial prefrontal cortex). They also appear to have reduced gray matter in regions of the brain associated with understanding other people's emotions. Hence, decreased amygdala and orbitofrontal cortex responses occur when given emotionally provocative stimuli. Therefore, we may hypothesize that if the amygdala doesn't function properly, it will influence these people's decision-making capabilities.[8] In other words, this weakened connection could partly explain the tendency of psychopaths to overvalue immediate rewards and neglect the consequences of imprudent or immoral behavior. Having this deficiency reduces the ability of these people to feel the distress experienced by their victims.

Ways of Prevention

Concerning the detection of white-collar crimes, *journalists* seem to be the primary detectors of these kinds of fraudulent activities, even more so than the standard law-enforcement agencies. The obvious explanation is

---

[8] Robert J. R. Blair (2010). Neuroimaging of Psychopathy and Antisocial Behavior: A Targeted Review, *Current Psychiatry Reports*, 12 (1), 76–82.

that the law-enforcement agencies generally cannot spare the large amount of time or resources required to unveil such crimes. In comparison, it often becomes the job of journalists and reporters to investigate these matters and uncover any deviations. All in all, however, whistleblowers tend to be the most important sources in detecting white-collar crimes. As they work inside these organizations, they have firsthand information about the crimes or fraud that are taking place. Most white-collar offenders have been detected by whistleblowers, who then tip off journalists and other authorities.

However, preventing white-collar crime from taking place would be a much better alternative than acting after the event. Bernard Madoff's $65 billion Ponzi scheme did raise serious public concerns about the effectiveness of regulatory oversight and due diligence. Not surprisingly, a white-collar crime like Madoff's triggered public outrage. Many people realized that someone who steals a small item from a convenience store could go to prison, while a white-collar criminal could get away with crimes that represent enormous costs to society. Madoff's exposure forced people to realize that there is no such thing as a victimless crime—and this applies not only to the direct victims of these crimes, but also to the families of the perpetrators. From the seizure and forfeiture of assets and huge tax fines to having a parent incarcerated, and the accompanying social stigma, the price tag of these crimes far outweighs any gains. The suicide of one of Madoff's sons and the estrangement of his wife are terrifying examples of one of the consequences of these criminal activities.

Notwithstanding the immense costs of these white-collar crimes, from a societal point of view, there is still not enough attention paid to their price tag. One reason often given is that many people don't feel their impact directly. The general public wants protection from "traditional" crimes, like theft, robbery, assault, rape, murder, and so on. These are viewed as tangible and familiar threats. In comparison, white-collar crimes seem less serious or injurious. Consequently, not enough resources are made available to deal with them—and white-collar criminals get away with it.

If preventive steps are taken, however, the "Fraud Diamond" can be a guide to help implement proactive measures to prevent white-collar crimes from happening in the first place.

Corporate Culture

As a starter, the prevailing corporate culture will play a central role. Leadership oversight and tone set at the top will be important enablers of an ethical, transparent culture and the foundation for effective corporate governance. An organization's leadership should make it very clear that ethics and compliance matter. In other words, they need to embed a culture of compliance in all decision-making processes. C-suite executives should have a zero tolerance for any form of "creative accounting." To facilitate compliance, open communication and transparency must be elements of the corporate culture. An environment of secrecy offers opportunities for potential white-collar crime—and any system that prefers profit over values is a very dangerous one indeed.

Leadership Development

Leadership development programs, 360-degree feedback systems, and regular surveys of employees can help those in charge of an organization make regular assessments to determine the ethical health of its corporate culture. These surveys can be highly effective ways to drive toxicity out of the organization. Leadership development programs can be considered early warning systems, assessing whether the culture of the organization is built on bedrock or on sand. Obtaining these data points can serve as a countervailing influence to prevent toxic practices from getting the upper hand—to prevent obsessing about good numbers on the balance sheet at all costs. In fact, playing these kinds of numbers games can have short-term benefits but will contribute to long-term disaster. In comparison, companies with a reputation for fairness and integrity—as reflected in satisfaction, climate, and leadership surveys—will do much better in the long run. They will have more satisfied employees, more loyal customers and suppliers—and will be more attractive to their investors. All in all, reputation is not only an output of profit and revenue but rather an equal function of the organization's ethical culture.

Entry and Exit

Of course, society and culture outside the office will also play a significant role in shaping people's personalities. With respect to entry, background checks and due diligence can play a vital role in preventing white-collar criminals from gaining traction. This implies that careful vetting of newcomers and well-designed organizational socialization programs should be par for the course. With respect to exit, if the process is conducted respectfully, exit interviews can provide honest feedback about any misconduct or toxicity within the organization. These exit interviews can also serve as an early warning system, signifying potential problem areas of which the organization could be unaware.

Control Systems

Well-designed internal reporting mechanisms are going to be a *sine qua non* for pre-empting white-collar crime. Tight financial control systems will be important to reduce opportunities for fraud. By establishing systems of control, inclusive of ethical standards, organizations can significantly reduce the financial and reputational risks associated with fraudulent activities. An obvious candidate for redesign is existing compensation systems. The design of these systems can have direct social and moral effects, not the least of which can be found in providing opportunities for exploitation, which is why executive compensation is a critical corporate governance issue. Ethics and compliance could be made elements of an organization's annual appraisal process. Organizations could even incentivize ambitious people by rewarding those who demonstrate commitment to their ethical values.

The Perfect Crime

The perfect crime is, of course, the crime that's never detected. Unfortunately, white-collar crime frequently comes into this category, going unnoticed or indeed not perceived as criminal at all. And even though it's said that crime doesn't pay, in many instances, white-collar crime seems to pay quite well. So, apart from preventive legal and organizational measures, a different level of prevention is called for. For example, business schools can play an important role in this. Their challenge is that the students they attract—those who will go on to lead organizations—already have a fully-fledged set of values by the time they arrive. Most ethics training occurs long before these students reach the classroom, it being transmitted by parents, other family members, friends, peers, and teachers. The values they have already internalized will be the bedrock of their behavior. Thus, teaching ethics at this level and at this stage in their career will be daunting at best and impossible at worst.

Nevertheless, something needs to be done, since, at the very least, many of the star players in these criminal dramas are graduates of business schools and were probably taught that a businessperson's only responsibility is to make money. Too many business schools teach only ROI, shareholder value, and maximization of profits, all of which are seen as incompatible with ethics, because ethics necessitates making sacrifices for the common good. Ethics in business requires organizational leaders to put the interests of others ahead of their own, which for all too many has been to maximize their pay packages.

Little by little, however, with the greater exposure of unethical business practices—and a better understanding of how they impact people in all walks of life—ethics has begun to play a more important role in business school education. But a designated ethics course isn't going to make much of a difference. Unless business school professors can inculcate a strong moral compass within their curriculums, it is highly unlikely that they will stop producing new robber barons. Business schools would be much more effective in preventing fraudulent behavior if they emphasized ethics and morals in every course and drove the point home with cautionary tales about the consequences of unethical behavior.

Fortunately, a new generation of leaders seem to be showing a change in their major concerns. They seem to be preoccupied with ethical decisions *and* bottom lines. To say that the only goal of a business enterprise is to maximize profit has become outdated. An increasing number of business leaders understand that profit cannot be the only goal if they want to engage the new generation of employees. Business schools as well are beginning to discover that they need to catch up with their students' world view. Happily, they are having to deal with fewer and fewer Gordon Gekkos and are now much less likely to have to tackle his assertion that "greed, for lack of a better word, is good." Clearly, however, it is people like Gekko who have no shame, a topic discussed in the next chapter.

5

The Dance Macabre of Shame

> Shame is a soul eating emotion.
> —Carl Gustav Jung

> Shame is the lie someone told you about yourself.
> —Anais Nin

Caroline, the head of HR at a large global retail chain, was confused. What to tell Liam, one of the sales directors in the company? What could she do to be helpful? It had become apparent that every time something went wrong, he felt compelled to blame himself. But why did he have this urge to always dig a hole for himself? This time, not surprisingly, he had decided to take the blame for a poor client presentation. But Caroline knew that the reality of what had happened was quite different. He wasn't the only one responsible. The presentation had been a team effort. Many other people had been involved. And even though it hadn't been a brilliant presentation, it had been quite an acceptable one. After all, the company did win the bid.

Caroline wondered why for Liam everything needed to be perfect. Why couldn't he accept the fact that mistakes were par for the course—that to make mistakes was human? Wasn't there some truth in the saying "People who don't make any mistakes, don't do anything"? Of course, it was quite understandable, when making a mistake, to feel somewhat down. But to keep on beating yourself up about it, was a very different story. And in this instance, Liam appeared to be so upset that after the incident he had even taken a sick leave. Wouldn't there be better ways of dealing with these situations? Wouldn't he be much better off if he would understand why he was feeling this way? Instead, every time when something went wrong, he created a self-reinforcing negative feedback loop with shame at its core.

Shame and the Human Condition

The story of Liam illustrates why it is important to pay attention to the role of shame in our lives. But as it is somewhat of a stealth emotion, it is very easily overlooked. Notwithstanding its hidden nature, however, all of us—psychopaths excluded—live with a modicum of shame. In fact, shame is part of the human condition. But when it becomes excessive, it will, as Carl Jung suggested, eat into our soul. Therefore, given its psychological impact, we should do all we can to protect ourselves from toxic shame.

The etymological root of shame seems to derive from the Proto-Indo-European word *kem*, meaning "to cover." The need to cover oneself appears to be a common reaction when dealing with shame. In fact, in the biblical story of Adam and Eve, much is made of their nakedness after they're thrown out of paradise. Furthermore, to continue this etymological journey, the word shame is also related to the Dutch and German verbs *schamen* or *schämen*, having to do with being disgraced and dishonored—not living up to the standards of the community. In addition, again taking an etymological perspective—referring to old Norse—shame also has to do with physiological responses, like the reddening of the cheeks.

The various meanings attributed to the word shame suggest how each person will experience this powerful emotion in slightly different ways. Truth be told, shame hides in many places. It is concealed behind guilt;

it hides behind anger; it can also appear as despair and depression. However, whatever the experience might be, almost always there will also be a physical, panic-like response. For example, common shame reactions include flushed cheeks, feelings of dizziness, tunnel vision, an inability to focus, a ringing in the ears, the constriction of the chest, and a reluctance to make eye contact. Furthermore, feelings of shame are often expressed by a covering gesture over the brow and eyes, a downcast gaze, or a slack posture.

As Liam's case illustrates, shame clouds good judgment, skews perception, and drives self-destructive behavior. Furthermore, referring to the latter, shame also hovers behind workaholism, perfectionism, and anything else that people compulsively do to make themselves feel better. In fact, people who are shame prone, as a form of compensation, try to cover up their perceived flaws by engaging in a long list of broken behaviors, including shaming others. What should also be noted is that very high levels of shame have been associated with more serious problems such as addictions, eating disorders, and even suicide.

When ashamed, people like Liam believe that their entire self is worthless. They feel powerless; they feel small. And the reason they think that way is that, in their imagination, they see themselves as being exposed to an audience that only exists for the purpose of confirming that they're no good. Unfortunately, these contorted mental acrobatics will suck the energy out of them. It makes them feel like damaged goods. In addition, what's also disturbing—taking an interpersonal perspective—is that people prone to toxic shame often defend themselves against these feelings by shaming others. Such behavior, however, only contributes to even more intense feelings of shame, creating an extremely destructive spiral. All in all, being haunted by shame has a profound negative effect on a person's psychological well-being. Therefore, this stealth emotion, if excessive, is at the core of much psychopathology. Mild to moderate feelings of shame, however, can be a force for the good in that it may guide people to live more ethical lives.

Shame vs. Guilt

Shame and guilt are two words often used almost interchangeably. But even though they both describe negative emotions, they refer to different experiences. To be more precise, in the case of shame, we are referring to the fear that we're not good enough—that we are inadequate. It arises from a negative evaluation of the self. In other words, the person that's a prisoner of shame is saying to him or herself, "I'm bad." In contrast, guilt comes from a negative evaluation of our behavior ("I have done something bad"). Thus, unlike guilt, which is the feeling of *having done* something wrong, shame is the feeling of *being* something wrong. It makes shame so much more difficult to overcome, as it pertains to the essence of the self. Thus, while people who are guilt prone are more likely to self-forgive, that wouldn't be the case for shame-prone people. In common parlance, however, shame and guilt often go hand in hand, a factor that can make both concepts quite confusing. In fact, the same action may give rise to feelings of both shame *and* guilt. Furthermore, to add to shame's complexity, it is possible to feel shame vicariously, that's to say to share the shame of another person or feel shame on his or her behalf, especially if this person is closely related, like a partner, sibling, or a child.

An Evolutionary Perspective

Given the pervasiveness of shame, we could ask ourselves what's the general purpose of this emotion? Why can it turn out to be such a powerful force? To answer this question, taking an evolutionary perspective, shame may have evolved under conditions where people's survival depended on whether they were abiding to specific group norms—when specific rules were needed to foster collaboration. In other words, shame may have helped to maintain the social order, reinforcing the idea that certain behaviors were harmful to the community. Thus, shame turned into an instrument for setting limits. It kept people in line by serving as an emotional course correction. And we can imagine how in Paleolithic times the need to follow certain rules would have been a matter of life and death. No wonder that if people were perceived as behaving shamefully, they were abandoned or sent into exile.

The Psychological Perspective

Taking more of a psychological developmental point of view, shame can be looked at as a complex emotional response that humans acquire during early childrearing. Shame comes to the fore at the developmental stage when emotional "imprinting" occurs. It refers to a period in time when children are completely dependent on the relationship with their caregivers. For example, we can observe how toddlers will mirror the positive and negative emotions of the mother. But if they're continually criticized, severely punished, neglected, abandoned, or in other ways mistreated, they quickly get the message that they are inadequate, inferior, or unworthy. If shame is excessively used as a major form of punishment, it will have a negative effect on the child's maturing brain, damaging the roots from which self-esteem grow. This parental disapproval becomes very hard to process and to digest. Consequently, these children will become shame prone, having internalized negative messages based on the perceptions and opinions of others. And little by little, these formative scars of childhood become part of their core being. As grown-ups, these people will feel inadequate; they never feel good enough.

As neuroscientists will also tell us, the more people engage in certain thoughts, the more they become prone to having these thoughts. In essence, these thoughts will turn into habits. No wonder that later in life, given the way these people have been treated, any form of criticism will go straight to the pit of their stomach. Each time they find themselves in situations that remind them of the negative experiences of their childhood, they feel as inadequate as they had when so labeled by their caregivers. And given the deep-seated roots of these emotions, these feelings will be hard to overcome. Shame-prone people end up with a low sense of self-esteem.

Overcoming Shame

Liam clearly had become someone who is shame prone. The challenge becomes how to make people like him feel more comfortable in their skin? How to make them less susceptible to shame?

Fortunately, there are ways of healing from toxic shame. Various steps can be taken to lessen shame's negative impact. Our personality has great plasticity—meaning that the capacity to change our brain's structure is well within the range of possibility. To be more specific, if we are prepared to explore different ways of dealing with life's challenges, we may discover new ways of thinking about ourselves. And if we experiment with different ways of thinking and behaving, it will help transform the neurological connections within our brain. Therefore, our challenge becomes finding ways to "reprogram" the minds of shame-prone people.

Returning to Liam, as it happened, after the incident described in the opening paragraphs of this chapter, Caroline obtained a greater understanding of why he was always so deeply affected by situations where something went wrong—why would he always take it so personally.

During a breakout session of a workshop that took place after the incident where both of them were participants, Caroline learned that Liam had grown up in an extremely dysfunctional family. Alcoholism had been one of his parents' major problems. Listening to Liam's story, she surmised that, within his family, he was the one most often put to shame. Whatever he would try to do, it never was good enough. Whenever something went wrong, both big and small, he was always the one to be blamed. Gradually, despite all his efforts trying to be the perfect child, he had become convinced that there was something very wrong with him. His particular upbringing led Liam to never see things as they really were. He never acquired a balanced perspective of what he was capable of. And if that wasn't already a heavy burden to carry, Caroline also understood that Liam often felt quite ashamed by the outrageous behavior of his parents.

Caroline learned how, later in life as an adult, Liam struggled to feel good about himself. He would always internalize and over-personalize everything done by him that wasn't perfect. To be more specific, for Liam, shame had turned into a toxic entity. Shame falsely was coloring his reality. The belief that he was always the only one responsible when mistakes were made came to define him. Day in and day out, critical voices inside his head would be judging and criticizing him, telling him that he was inadequate, inferior, in other words, not good enough.

1. *To Acknowledge That There Is a Problem*

If Liam reminds you of yourself, meaning that you are also quite shame prone, the first step you should take in trying to change your outlook is to acknowledge that toxic shame is at the core of whatever your problems may be. Of course, doing so, is not going to be easy. Shame is a very difficult emotion to deal with. Even if, from a rational perspective, you know that your concerns are baseless, it still will be hard to talk about it. Shame tends to be a subject that isn't easy to acknowledge. Furthermore, even if you are prepared to do so, you may not even be consciously aware that you're shame prone. Shame isn't an easy emotion to detect. And its detection becomes even more complicated as shame—as mentioned before—shows itself in many disguises. But by acknowledging that you have a toxic shame problem, you will have taken a first step. You will have decided that shame no longer should define you. You are willing to bring this problem into the open. And what's worthwhile knowing is that the less you talk about shame, the more power it will have over your life. Isn't it very true that a wound that's never been exposed will never heal? You need to acknowledge what's happening to you.

2. *Sharing the Problem*

The next step in coping with shame is to share the problem. It is more difficult for shame to survive if you can share your story with an empathic person. For example, as we saw in Liam's case, under the right circumstances, he was prepared to talk about his feelings and his personal history. Yet, even though he had mentioned to Caroline how feelings of shame contributed to his sense of inadequacy, the question remained as to whether he had done sufficient self-analysis. Had he really explored how he would enter this self-punishing, downward cycle when something went wrong? Did he understand why an emotional wave would wash over him that would cloud his thinking? Did he recognize how he would get stuck in a spiral of unworthiness, making him feel totally inadequate? During Caroline's discussions with Liam, it became very clear that the degree to which he felt compelled to hide those aspects of himself from others—even going as far as to hide them from himself—was very much dependent on the intensity of those shameful feelings.

After Liam had told his story, incomplete as it might have been, Caroline explained to him that everyone is prone to shame; that he isn't alone with these feelings. It is part of the human condition. But even though shame is a universal experience, nobody likes to talk about it. In that respect, Caroline told Liam he had made a very good start by explaining his feelings. She added that the less you talk about your feelings of shame, the greater the power they will have over you. Talking about it, accepting that shame is part of the human condition, would be the way to start a personal healing process. It would help Liam to cope with these shameful feelings without resorting to destructive measures such as masking its pain with drugs or alcohol or lashing out at other people. In acting this way, he wouldn't be giving into shame's message that he is indeed bad. Thus, by experimenting with a different way of thinking, Liam could begin to feel more confident and genuine.

3. *Looking for Origins*

Also, Caroline explained to Liam, he should try to better understand where these shameful feelings came from. For example, how did he think it all started? What would have been at the roots? Were there any people in his life who would set off this shame reflex? And why were they able to do so? Furthermore, in what way was he perpetuating these shameful feelings? These would be the kinds of questions Liam should ask himself to better understand what was happening to him.

In case you have similar reactions as Liam, you should realize that these negative self-evaluations have their roots in messages that you've received from others, especially the messages given to you during your formative years. Your caregivers may set you up for shame when you didn't live up to their expectations. Unfortunately, by putting you down, they have planted the seeds of shame. You may have internalized their voices. And these inner critics—these voices in your head—may be continuing to tell that you're not good enough. They may keep on feeding you shame-based messages and interpretations of your daily life. And given your personal history, not much is needed to awaken these inner critics.

4. *Recognizing the Signs*

In addition, when you feel shame entering you, you should try to understand what's happening to you before these shameful feelings take hold. By being aware of what your shame triggers are, you can help nip this downward shame spiral in the bud. But it also means that you need to identify the physical signs that accompany this downward shame spiral. You need to figure out what negative physical and emotional effects shame is having on you. For example, where in your body do you feel the shame? What kind of emotional reactions do you have? You should try to identify your default reactions when you feel ashamed.

Toxic shame is what makes you feel small and worthless. It is what locks you into a painful loop of negative self-talk. Indications that toxic shame is getting at you is when you enter an inner dialogue of self-doubt, when you are saying things to yourself like, "I'm not good enough," "I'm stupid," "I'm worthless," "Why can't I behave like other people," or "Why have I done this?" Naturally, these inner dialogues are going to be slightly different for everyone. In addition, they are often accompanied by physical reactions. Toxic shame will open the door to anger, self-disgust, and other less-than-desirable feelings. Furthermore, another indicator of being in the pangs of shame is that you're becoming not only highly critical of yourself but also critical of other people. Quite often, people who are shame prone, see their own faults mirrored in their family members, friends, co-workers, or other people. They will be tempted to react negatively toward them.

But if you become aware of your typical knee-jerk reactions concerning shame, you will increase your chances of taking time out to engage in greater self-reflection. If so, it will help you to become acquainted with your specific shame triggers so that you can respond in a more constructive manner. All in all, you need to become attuned to your inner dialogue. You need to expand your capacity to observe first what's happening to you and not immediately act on it.

5. *Learn to Forgive Yourself*

In overcoming toxic shame the most essential internal shift requires that you separate what you do from your sense of self-worth. In short, you need to practice seeing *what you do* and *who you are* as being two different things. You should remind yourself that you are so much more than your actions. In addition, it is important to realize that so many things about you are within your control, the implication being that instead of giving into these shame triggers, you need to ban them from your life. You need to embrace who you are rather than struggling to fulfill an outside notion of who you should be. In other words, if you realize that your whole identity isn't on the line when something doesn't work out, you'll be much freer to create and to take risks. You will be able to look at both praise and condemnation with the perspective that it deserves. You will be able to digest critical reactions and move on. You will judge yourself less harshly for things you have done. And once you realize what these inner critics are doing to you, you will be able to argue with these internalized parts of yourself. You will be able to find alternative explanations when things don't work out. You will be able to forgive yourself for being human, realizing that many other people are struggling with similar issues.

Forgiving means moving on, not to get stuck in the past, even though you can always learn from this past. And while you are in this forgiving mode, you may be able to differentiate between what you are feeling and what you should be feeling. Such an inner dialogue will help you to move forward, to become a newer and better version of yourself. It will help you to get out of this downward shame spiral, to move onto a more constructive path. Conversely, if you define yourself by what others think about you, you are putting the power of your life in the hands of these other people.

Forgiving implies cultivating self-compassion—embracing who you are. You should treat yourself in the same respectful way in which you are treating people you really care about. This other oriented pattern should be the framework of how to develop compassion for yourself. Therefore, any time the inner voice of self-doubt comes to the fore, you should consider it a warning that it's time to reframe the situation. You need to tame these inner critics. You need to make sure that the voice of positivity becomes louder than the voice of self-doubt. It means cultivating an alternative dialogue centered on self-acceptance. After all, as a human being, you're imperfect like everyone else. Therefore, every time you enter this process of self-blame or even blaming others, analyze what's happening to you, stop criticizing, forgive yourself and others, and move on. Try to make shaming a behavior pattern that's simply unacceptable.

6. *Finding Professional Help*

As mentioned before, to get beyond shame means acknowledging it and sharing these feelings with trusted people. As Liam discovered, sharing parts of his life story with Caroline turned out to be a life changer. Clearly, the empathic reaction of Caroline helped him to acquire a more realistic perspective vis-à-vis shame. It made him realize that there was no shame in being wrong. What was wrong, however, was not doing anything about it—not reframing the experience. For example, during their discussions, Caroline told Liam that if one of his direct reports would have bombed the presentation, wouldn't he have been supportive? Wouldn't he have said, "You tried hard, but you were just too anxious," or "You'll do much better next time"?

These interchanges helped Liam to understand the origins of his toxic shame—how it had affected his sense of self-esteem—how it would contribute to dysfunctional behavior. In fact, in helping him to come up with strategies for dealing with these feelings, Caroline had taken on the role of coach. She had helped him understand how much he tended to resort to negative thinking and how a negative thought spiral could then get the upper hand. Liam came to understand the extent to which shame had been tapping into his threat defense system while ignoring his caregiving system. Thus, by pushing Liam to embark on these "corrective emotional experiences," Caroline helped him to improve his sense of self-esteem, fostering a greater sense of self-acceptance, and reducing his unhealthy reactions to shame.

Of course, authentic sharing requires vulnerability which can be quite anxiety inducing—especially if you're discussing a subject you don't like to talk about. Therefore, if your wounds are deep enough, if you're like Liam, you might want to ask a coach or psychotherapist for assistance. People in the helping professions can be skilled at guiding you in such an inward bound journey. They can assist you in discovering the origins of shame-like experiences, encouraging you to explore your inner critics for the purpose of arriving at a different dialogue. If you're able to do so, most likely, you will obtain a greater sense of control over your life, being less prone to shame reactions.

A Master Emotion

As has been said before, shame is part of the human experience. To feel shame is to be human. It can be considered Homo sapiens' master emotion, the fear that we're not good enough. Much of shame's power comes from it being seemingly unspeakable. It is an emotion that most of us don't like to talk about. But everyone, save psychopaths, will have shame experiences. But, if we can keep our feelings of shame within boundaries—if we can prevent the harmful tendency to self-blame—we will be able to make peace with this shadow side. To realize that we're good enough, worthwhile, and deserving of love and acceptance will be essential in living our most authentic life. Unfortunately, shame is not the only feeling that holds us back in the art of living. Procrastination is another example of a coping mechanism that has gone wrong, as will be made quite clear in the following chapter.

6

Catching the Thief of Time: The Perils of Procrastination

> *It is not because things are difficult that we do not dare, it is because we do not dare that they are difficult.*
> —Seneca
>
> *When you have to make a choice and don't make it, that in itself is a choice.*
> —William James
>
> *Tomorrow is often the busiest day of the week.*
> —Spanish Proverb

Introduction

Victor was wondering what to do. His subordinates were pushing him to make up his mind about a major acquisition, but he was unsure how to proceed. Should he go ahead with it or not? He knew that the clock was ticking, but he was worried about the downside. What if the promised synergies didn't materialize? What if they would be buying a cat-in-the-sack? In the meantime, the constant pressure to make a decision was wearing him down. He felt low and exhausted, due, no doubt, to his insomnia. He lay awake at night, thinking about all the things that could go wrong.

Victor was reluctant to admit it to himself, but he had long had a problem responding to difficult tasks and decisions. He would always put them off. Maybe this was why he hadn't really taken a deep dive into the details of the acquisition. Overthinking and procrastination were his habitual *modus operandi*. He was very good at finding distractions, doing things that were more satisfying. He could always convince himself that more information was necessary to make a truly informed decision. However, he was well aware of the saying, "When there's a hill to climb, don't think that waiting will make it smaller." Although he knew he shouldn't prevaricate and delay, he felt as if he couldn't help himself. Why did he feel incapable of making a decision? Was he really waiting for the right moment? Would that moment ever come?

Sadly, although procrastination can offer relief from unpleasant tasks, the relief is only temporary. Putting off dealing with something only makes matters worse, as the "Victors" of this world find out the hard way. And there are many of them: it is estimated that approximately 20 percent of US men and women are chronic procrastinators.[1]

The Procrastinator Test

Does Victor's behavior sound familiar to you? Do you share his tendencies? To find out, ask yourself the following questions:

- Do you quickly feel overwhelmed after being assigned a task?
- When faced with a major assignment, do you tend to focus on nonessential activities instead of what needs to be done?
- Are you very easily distracted?
- Do you often wait until the last moment to do things?
- Do you rarely finish projects on time?
- Do you tend to live from deadline to deadline?
- Do you often hope that if you ignore a task, it will just go away?
- Are you good in finding excuses for not doing something?

---

[1] https://www.apa.org/news/press/releases/2010/04/procrastination

- Do you have a lengthy to-do list?
- Do you tend to be late for appointments?

A procrastinator will answer "Yes" to most of these questions.

Contributing Variables to Procrastination

Etymologically, procrastination is derived from the Latin *procrastinare*—to put things off until tomorrow—and the ancient Greek *akrasia*—doing something against your better judgment. However, procrastination is more than simply putting things off or deciding not to act; it is also a failure of self-regulation, in other words, a coping mechanism that's gone haywire. While delaying doing something can temporarily make us feel better, the feeling will not last. In fact, procrastination contributes to several negative emotions, not the least of which are shame and guilt. For extreme procrastinators, however, these negative feelings are just additional reasons to put things off for longer, until this self-defeating behavior becomes a form of self-harm. The longer an individual avoids a task, the more difficult it becomes to break the dark cycle of procrastination.

Habitual procrastination can have a negative effect on a person's mental and physical health, causing depression in some cases, which further aggravates the situation. Like Victor, procrastinators may end up lacking the energy to start or finish even the simplest tasks. Procrastination is also an indicator of self-doubt; insecurity about their ability to tackle an assignment is yet another reason to put it off or to work on other, less challenging assignments. No wonder that procrastination jeopardizes both personal and professional relationships, leading to resentment among friends, family members, and colleagues, whether it involves major acquisitions or unpaid bills and missed income tax returns. So why do people procrastinate? What prevents them from taking action?

Many conscious and unconscious factors can explain why some people procrastinate. A rather obvious one is that procrastinators put off doing a specific task either because they fear they won't like doing it or that it won't be pleasurable enough to override something else they could do. Another factor could be that they fear they won't do the task very well. They may feel overwhelmed by the complexity of the assignment. For example, going back to Victor, maybe he just wasn't up to dealing with acquisitions. Or maybe his exhaustion meant he simply didn't have the energy to take on yet another challenging assignment. Maybe he lacked the motivation to act because the rewards tied up with the acquisition lay too far in the future. If there is a significant gap between the time when a task needs to be completed and the time it takes to get any reward for completing it, the value of the reward tends to be discounted. Basically, when making long-term decisions, we don't feel that strong a connection with our future self. Even if we recognize intellectually that putting off a task will create future stress, our brains are still wired to be more concerned with removing a present threat. Actually, from an evolutionary point of view, Homo sapiens wasn't really designed to think far ahead because we needed to focus on providing for ourselves in the here-and-now. Hence, an individual like Victor may not experience a great sense of urgency to get things done. To make things worse, we are even less able to make thoughtful, future-oriented decisions when we feel stressed.

Another, less obvious and more unconscious impediment that may stop Victor from acting could be a fear of failure, that he might do something wrong, that the acquisition will not work well, that his board of directors will give him negative feedback. Given all the conscious (and unconscious) thoughts passing through his mind, the one shouting loudest might be "I don't want to do it." In essence, Victor is failing to self-regulate. When we need to make a decision or complete a task, we usually rely on our self-control to push ourselves to get things done. Victor, however, is postponing things unnecessarily, even while he knows he shouldn't be doing so.

One of the drivers that motivates us to take action—that is, why we might decide to exert self-control—is the expectation that we will reap the benefits for our efforts in the future. Normally, due to these intrapsychic calculations, we execute certain things in a timely manner. But procrastinators can't do this. Instead, their inability to self-regulate creates a downward spiral of negative emotions that deters future efforts. Initially, not doing something they're supposed to do brings illusory benefits—the temporary pleasure of not doing what's perceived as an unpleasant task. But in avoiding doing something perceived as unpleasant in the present, they're setting the stage for having to pay a much higher price in the future for their inaction.

Furthermore, while procrastinators may initially experience a sense of control over their lives by not taking action, this rapidly dissolves into feelings of lack of control, as time constraints begin to restrict their ability to successfully execute the assignment. This comedy of judgmental errors is aggravated by self-deception. Some procrastinators believe they perform better under pressure. But last-minuters often produce second-rate results. Procrastination is also driven by other factors, an important one being rebelliousness. The procrastinator may have problems with authority and letting a deadline slip can be a way of adding drama to their lives.

Character Types

Many procrastinators tend to be perfectionists for whom it may be psychologically more acceptable never to tackle a job than to face the possibility of not doing it well. Generally speaking, however, certain personality types are more likely to become procrastinators. For example, procrastination is more common among people with obsessive-compulsive disorder (OCD), the reason being that OCD is often linked to maladaptive, unhealthy perfectionism, which contributes to anxiety about making mistakes, doubts about whether what's being done is done correctly, and worries about other people's expectations. Hence, as procrastinators are highly concerned about what others will think of them, they will put their future at risk to avoid being judged. People with attention-deficit hyperactivity disorder (ADHD) can also struggle with procrastination. As they are quickly distracted by outside stimuli as well as intrusive thoughts, it will be difficult for them to start an assignment, especially if it is difficult or doesn't seem to be very interesting. And then there are people who have passive-aggressive behavior patterns. Even though they may appear pleasant, or even cheerful on the outside, beneath this veneer they experience feelings of anger and resentment when asked to do something. As they have conflictual relationships with authority figures, they resort to more indirect ways to show how they really feel, like putting off finishing a task that's requested by others or making deliberate mistakes.

In other words, there's a disconnect between what a passive-aggressive person says and what he or she really does.

In contrast, non-procrastinators focus on whatever needs to be done. They have a greater sense of inner security and are less preoccupied with what others think of them than how they feel about themselves. People who score low on procrastination tend to be high on the personality trait known as conscientiousness, one of the broad dispositions identified by the "Big Five Theory of Personality."[2] People who score high on conscientiousness also tend to have high scores in other areas, including self-discipline, persistence, and personal responsibility.

Behavioral Recommendations

There are many drivers that contribute to procrastination, among which low self-confidence and a high level of anxiety are prominent. Procrastination is also linked to rumination, repeatedly having the same, dark, negative thoughts. As Victor's example shows, procrastination and rumination could also be signs of depression. Depression is depleting; drained of energy, you will have a hard time planning ahead or following through. "What's the point?" and "Why bother?" will become familiar thoughts. Notwithstanding these complex intrapsychic processes, it's possible to overcome procrastination, although it will be a real challenge. Changing habitual behavior patterns consumes a lot of psychic energy as it means getting out of your comfort zone. It also means that you need to engage in *reframing* and *self-compassion*.

One way of embarking on a change process is to engage in a structured regimen of behavioral interventions. In the short term, several cognitive "tricks" can help prevent procrastination from getting the upper hand.

---

[2] Robert R. McCrae and Paul T. Costa, (1990). *Personality in Adulthood*. New York: Guilford.

Too Big a Task

You may think that what needs to be done is completely overwhelming. You tell yourself that the task is too big, so you postpone getting started. But the fact is that the time wasted *not* getting started is the biggest waste of time of all. Therefore, the way to make a task appear more doable is to reframe it by breaking it up into several small parts that you tackle one at a time. Try not to think about the remaining tasks. Instead, start by trying to complete the first one. Even though this could be seen as a form of self-deception, it will give you a better perspective on the task and make it seem more manageable. Small progressive steps will make you feel much better about the assignment and better about yourself, which will reduce the desire to procrastinate. If this form of behavioral reframing gets you started, motivation will follow.

Lack of Self-Control

You are more likely to overcome issues with self-control and complete your assignment if you set yourself deadlines. So, the next time you have a big assignment that needs to be done, try not only to break it down into smaller parts but also to set a time and date for delivering each part. It will help you to stay focused and it is more likely that things will get done. In other words, setting deadlines undermines procrastination. In addition, just by taking action, by doing something about the situation, you will reduce your stress level. And while considering stress management, if you are expected to accomplish a number of tasks during a specific period, it's also helpful to start with the most difficult one. You will feel so much better if you tackle the most important task of the day immediately, even if it's the hardest. Subsequently, the easier tasks will seem to take care of themselves.

Time Management

You might have been tempted to put things off, thinking that you have all the time in the world. Realizing that you no longer have time, you may find yourself scrambling to get things done and your stress levels skyrocket. If this happens often to you, you are clearly not setting aside enough time for a task. Maybe you're overly optimistic about what you can do. Maybe you're deluding yourself about your abilities. Consistently underestimating time commitments can make you procrastinate more than you would normally do. Delaying acting is simply a trap. You will always be able to find another reason to put something off. The way to get started is to stop talking and start doing, managing your time more realistically.

Recognize Busyness

It can be very satisfying to organize the papers on your desk and see the results of your work there and then. It can be quite enjoyable, frittering away time on trivial pursuits rather than getting on with work-related projects. But what you are actually doing is filling your days with busyness to avoid getting down to business. Of course, you can rationalize your reluctance to begin. You can tell yourself that not everything is ready. But as the Russian novelist Ivan Turgenev once wrote, "If we wait for the moment when everything, absolutely everything is ready, we shall never begin." One way of getting out of this delaying tactic is to make a to-do list. Obviously, such a list is not the be-and-end-all. However, writing down what needs to be done can have a wonderful effect on your mental state and will often galvanize you into action. To help you to stay on track, you might consider putting a due date next to each item on the list or go one step further and prioritize. Concentrate on the three most important items that need your attention. As an old Portuguese proverb goes, "Think of many things but start with one."

Have Some Fun

While following these recommendations, you should also keep in mind that the time you enjoy wasting isn't always wasted time. We all need variety and relaxation. So, intersperse your work with rewards, relaxation, and celebration of tasks completed. It will make it easier to continue working on what still needs to be done and will help you to fight procrastination. It is important to remember that life is more than to-do lists. It helps to create "feel good" experiences and to be nice to yourself. Make it a habit to pat yourself on your back when you finish an item on your to-do list on time. Congratulate yourself on work well done. And the obvious way of congratulating yourself is to create fun moments.

What's Happening Under the Surface?

An assignment left undone remains undone in two places: one is the assignment itself, the other is inside your head. And it is the latter that will use up your energy. Not doing something can be exhausting. It will gnaw at your conscience. It will make you feel ashamed and guilty. There is more to procrastination than what is immediately obvious. Even though the behavioral measures suggested here can be helpful, there are also daunting unconscious forces at work.

Perfectionism

Chronic procrastinators tend to be extremely hard on themselves, before and after an assignment. Many of them strive for perfection. In fact, it is fair to say that perfectionism can be the mother of procrastination. Many procrastinators set impossible standards for themselves and put off what needs to be done out of fear of not being able to complete a task perfectly. This behavior can be associated with self-criticism and a lack of self-compassion accompanied by feelings of anxiety. These people imagine that something awful will happen if they don't execute an assignment perfectly.

Once they start to feel anxious, their negative thoughts start to snowball, contributing to a vicious circle of negativity. Eventually, their negative thoughts will leave them feeling tense, tired, and even hopeless, wondering whether they will ever get off this negative treadmill. Consequently, anxious at taking on the assignment, they resort to procrastination as a way to give their brain temporary relief. But the assignment won't go away. It keeps on troubling them, creating more emotional turmoil. Yet the extremely high standards they set for themselves stop them moving forward. Paralyzed by perfectionism, they don't see that it is unworkable, impractical, and irrational.

A lack of self-confidence plays a role in this equation. Fearful of being judged is yet another reason why people look for an excuse to procrastinate. Unfortunately, the combination of perfectionism and lack of self-confidence is the ideal mix to create fear of failure. Consequently, these people tell themselves (not necessarily consciously) that they can't fail at something if they don't do it at all. But although they may imagine that they have more control over their lives by putting things off, this feeling quickly dissolves when they begin to experience a lack of control as time constraints begin to restrict their ability to make effective decisions.

So, if you feel tempted to put things off or delay completing an assignment simply because you're worried that the outcome will be less than perfect, it is high time for you to face your demons and confront your fear of failure. The assignment isn't going away. So, the next time you find yourself thinking about putting something off simply to avoid potential failure, you should tackle it head on. Failure is a part of life. Everyone makes mistakes. Nobody realistically expects perfection from you.

Once you get an assignment done, even if the outcome is less than ideal, you might feel more confident in your ability to complete tasks. You should tell yourself that an imperfectly executed task is better than an uncompleted task. Of course, your anxiety level will rise temporarily when you take risks in decision-making. Again, try to manage it. It is important to reframe your perspectives if you want to overcome these fears. Basically, you need to learn to be nicer to yourself. You need to learn the power of self-compassion.

A Highly Critical Superego

If you tend to be a procrastinator, you may be plagued by an internal "enemy," a relentlessly self-critical, internal voice that reminds you of your failings and shortcomings. In other words, you may have an extremely demanding conscience that fuels your perfectionistic behavior. A major reason could be that you were raised by highly critical parents. If that was the case, their critical voices are now part of you. They have been internalized. As a result, you may have developed a harsh, fault-finding superego, and become extremely hard on yourself—self-judging and self-critical. You catastrophize. You will have a tendency to define yourself on the basis of a single outcome, thinking, for example, "If I mess up this assignment, I will be a total failure." Consequently, you will fret about the assignment and how difficult it will be to complete it successfully.

Because your harsh superego is so emotionally draining, you may feel you lack the energy required to complete the assignment. But if you feel that way, you need to change your way of looking at yourself, and create a more benign, supportive self-observing conscience. You need to reframe the way you look at the world, including the way you look at the assignments given to you. Try to consider the positive aspects of any challenging task you are given. In particular, try to be more self-forgiving.

Self-forgiveness will allow you to move past your maladaptive behavior and focus on the future without the burden of past actions. It implies treating yourself with kindness and understanding in the face of your mistakes and failures. And by exercising self-compassion, you create a buffer against possible negative reactions when things don't work out as expected. Self-compassion also means that you meet your challenges with greater acceptance rather than destructive rumination and regrets. Self-compassion will reduce the psychological distress that is an enabler of procrastination. It will boost your motivation, enhance your feelings of self-worth, and foster positive emotions like optimism, curiosity, and personal initiative.

However, to be able to employ self-compassion requires you to become more self-aware. Every time you put yourself down—every time you judge yourself harshly—you need to pay attention. This kind of emotional labor can be difficult to do alone, especially as your harsh superego is adept at getting at you in any number of unconscious ways. Discussing this kind of behavior pattern with a non-judgmental, supportive, understanding person, like a friend or family member, will make you more aware of it. You might discover that it is helpful simply to get your feelings out into the open. It can also be a highly effective way to ameliorate your level of anxiety. As you become more self-aware, you will recognize when you are being hard on yourself. This recognition will enable you to step back and take a more compassionate view. And the more you become aware of your harsh superego, the more empowered you will be to change it.

Self-compassion also implies recognizing your common humanity. You need to realize that you're not alone in having these kinds of problems. We all have the same failings and virtues. Knowing this will lighten the burden, especially when it comes to thinking about your faults. Being mindful, paying attention to the present moment as often as you can, also has a part to play in the self-compassion equation. Even though it is important to recognize how your past influences your present behavior, continuing to harp on it is unhelpful. Instead, you should try to look forward to how you can create a better future.

In more serious cases, if, for example, your procrastination has become a chronic or debilitating issue, it could be symptomatic of severe psychological problems, and you may need the help of a coach or psychotherapist. Such helping professionals can make you more aware of specific habits and thoughts that lead to procrastination. They can help you evaluate your personal goals, strengths, weaknesses, and priorities. They can point out self-defeating problems such as your fears, anxieties, difficulties in concentrating, poor time management, indecisiveness, and perfectionism. They can help you discipline yourself in setting priorities. They can also help you to follow behavioral interventions such as those suggested earlier. Most of all, they can help you reframe the way you look at things.

Over time, the *modus operandi* of compassionate and empathetic therapists or coaches can be internalized, replacing your harsh superego with a more benign and supportive one. Should Victor turn to helping professionals, he might learn from them that his procrastination is a form of self-destruction—a strategy of self-sabotage whereby the displacement activities he uses to avoid completing an assignment use up more time and energy than the assignment itself would. Or as the famous psychologist William James once said, "Nothing is so fatiguing as the eternal hanging on of an uncompleted task."

The people in the chapter that follows, however, are not into procrastination. On the contrary, they tend to be action oriented. I am referring to the people able to amass great fortunes: the super-rich. In Chapter 7, I will discuss some of the factors that made them so successful.

7

The Inner Theater of the Super-Rich

> *Fortune sides with him who dares.*
> —Virgil
>
> *There are people who have money and people who are rich.*
> —Coco Chanel
>
> *The way to become rich is to put all your eggs in one basket and then watch that basket.*
> —Andrew Carnegie

Introduction

Reading about the activities of Jeff Bezos, I cannot help but wonder how it feels to have been the richest man in the world. I mean not just rich but *seriously rich*. What might you ask yourself, having accumulated so much money, about what to do with it? Of course, given Bezos' incredible wealth, he can certainly afford to spend it on a few trinkets. When your estimated worth is $135 billion, one could argue that you deserve to have a superyacht at the modest price of $500 million. I'm sure his yacht is an eye catcher. In fact, a recent *BBC News* article noted that the yacht "is almost as big as the Great Pyramid of Giza (if the vessel was laid out vertically). It's just under half as long as the Eiffel Tower."[1] But why not? Most likely, to be the owner of such a yacht is much cheaper than one of Bezos' other expensive hobbies, like shooting rockets into the air. In fact, he is doing what many seriously rich people have done before him. Thanks to people like them, the world is now full of cathedrals, mosques, and mausoleums.

Studying the history of these super-rich businesspeople, it appears that John D. Rockefeller, the father of the petroleum industry, in the early years of the previous century, became the world's first billionaire. He lived in a period of time when various entrepreneurs took advantage of the new technologies to amass great fortunes, a trend that has continued to this day. While the likes of John D. Rockefeller, John Pierpont Morgan, Andrew Carnegie, and Henry Ford created enormous fortunes, a century later some of the privileged few have repeated their achievement. Taking a closer look at how they acquired their wealth, the greatest fortunes have been made in the finance and investments, manufacturing and technology sectors. Interestingly enough, the places that have turned out to be most advantageous for becoming seriously rich are the emerging economies like Russia and China. For budding entrepreneurs, these countries have offered tremendous opportunities. There is something to be said about being lucky enough to be in the right place, at the right time.

Presently, there is more extraordinary wealth creation than ever before. Still, to become part of this billionaire club remains an exclusive proposition. Notwithstanding its exclusivity, *Forbes* suggests that currently there are 2668 billionaires worldwide. Europe, the US, and some Asia-Pacific nations account for most of these extremely wealthy people.[2] And as a signal of the seriousness of the issue, it is estimated that by 2030, the richest 1 percent of the population is on target to own two-thirds of the world's wealth.[3]

Taking a hard look at these contemporary billionaires, most of them didn't start out this way. In fact, the number of self-made billionaires has

---

[1] https://www.bbc.com/news/world-us-canada-57079327

[2] https://www.forbes.com/sites/chasewithorn/2022/04/05/forbes-36th-annual-worlds-billionaires-list-facts-and-figures-2022

[3] https://www.theguardian.com/business/2018/apr/07/global-inequality-tipping-point-2030

overtaken the multi-generational ones. As it happens, people with inherited wealth have given way to the more entrepreneurial types. Looking at their business history, most of them made their money through useful inventions (examples are Steve Jobs, Bill Gates, and Elon Musk). Others found innovative ways to solve problems (think of Mark Zuckerberg, Travis Kalanick, or Jack Ma). And yet others appeared to be great investors (Warren Buffett being among the most famous ones).

Becoming a Billionaire

Can you be a billionaire? Do you have what it takes? Or is there something special about these people that makes them not like you and me? The writer F. Scott Fitzgerald thought so. He once said, "Let me tell you about the very rich. They are different from you and me." He imagined that they think, make decisions, and react differently than other people. Therefore, could it be true that these people possess a mysterious X-factor that makes them so extremely successful? Do billionaires have other things in common than merely their heady bank accounts? Could it be more than just timing and luck? Thus, the question becomes: if you would like to become part of this billionaire club, what's needed to get there?

The historian Rainer Zitelmann tried to deal with this question in his study about the wealth elite.[4] To find answers, he interviewed 45 members of this exclusive club, mostly self-made entrepreneurs with net assets (granted only) between 30 million and 1 billion euros. What also limited this study's scope, however, was the fact that all of the participants were of German nationality. But apart from just interviewing these people, to give the study more depth, Zitelmann managed to have them go through a psychological exercise. He used the Big Five personality test as a way of figuring out whether specific personality traits played a key role in the successful pursuit of wealth.[5]

---

[4] Rainer Zitelmann (2018). *The Wealth Elite: A Groundbreaking Study of the Psychology of the Super Rich*. London: LID Publishing.
[5] Robert R. McCrae and Paul T. Costa, (1990). *Personality in Adulthood*. New York: Guilford.

The Big Five model in psychology that has dominated much thinking about personality suggests that behavior is determined by people's degree of neuroticism, conscientiousness, extraversion, openness to experience, and agreeableness.[6] Unfortunately, looking at the findings of these tests, Zitelmann's results weren't exactly earth-shattering. He discovered that the very rich, from a *neuroticism* point of view, tended to be quite stable. Also, they appeared to be *extraverted* (or knew how to present themselves that way). Furthermore, they tended to be more *open to new experiences*. In addition, they were less *agreeable*, meaning that it was less likely that they would shy away from conflicts. And finally, according to this study, the very rich seemed to be quite *conscientious*, implying they were more detail oriented. In other words, they were very thorough concerning the completion of tasks.

Clearly, what this study points out is that these super-rich may be somewhat different from you and me, but not by much. It is also possible, however, that the reason that these findings weren't really earth-shattering was because Zitelmann didn't analyze his subjects sufficiently in depth. He may not have explored the inner theater of these people deeply enough. Of course, what should be said in his defense is that making generalizations about certain types of people isn't easy. Not all rich people are the same, while the same could be said about all poor people.

The Inner Theater

All in all, the question remains: "What is the personality profile of these super-rich?" To that we might add: "Do you have what it takes to become a member of this club?" As I have been dealing with quite a few of them given my work as an executive coach, psychoanalyst, and management professor, let me make a few observations.

To start with, billionaires are different from the more run-of-the-mill corporate executives in that working for a corporation isn't the road

---

[6] Paul T. Costa, Jr., & Robert R. McCrae (1988). Personality in adulthood: A six-year longitudinal study of self-report and spouse ratings on the NEO Personality Inventory, *Journal of Personality and Social Psychology*, 54, 853–863.

toward membership into this exclusive club. If you are working for somebody—if you are dependent on pay checks—it is very unlikely that you will become super-rich. Most of the very wealthy earned their money not through what they earned from a job but from starting a business. To end up as a billionaire is all about self-employment, in other words, entrepreneurship.

Continuing this more "on the surface" description of these people, most of these self-made billionaires come from seemingly normal, middle-class backgrounds. They appeared to have been raised by parents who encouraged them to pursue their interests. But quite early in life, for many different "below the surface" reasons (I'm referring to various unconscious dynamics), these budding super-rich realized the importance of having control over their lives. Due to the prevailing family dynamics, they had become somewhat "allergic" toward authority figures. To work under somebody had become a very unattractive proposition. Therefore, for many of these people, independence became all-important. In addition, while growing up, many of them would become intrigued by entrepreneurial role models. The examples they admired could have been a family member or some other person that would play an important role in their imagination. It made them decide that they would like to become like them. Furthermore, what should be added, while growing up, again for various "below the surface" reasons, they came to appreciate the importance of having money. For example, it might very well be that during their childhood there wasn't much money to go around. Consequently, early in life, they realized what money could bring, that money can make money, that money would bring independence, and that money would bring them freedom. As a matter of fact, many of their activities during their youth showed how important making money had become for them. Quite early in life, many of these people would find ways to make some money.

That being said about their personal history, these super-rich also have a number of other behavioral themes in common. The question is, do you fit the bill?

(1) Many of these self-made billionaires possess a somewhat different *Weltanschauung* compared to run-of-the-mill businesspeople.

They're very focused and they tend to be people with big ideas. And with these big ideas come big-picture thinking. In addition, they're the kinds of people that can envision possible futures. What should be added is that they're quite driven and have lots of energy. Business-focused as they are, they seem to be enthralled with a *magnificent obsession*. In other words, they are investing their body and soul in whatever vision they have for the future. It is this intense focus of what they want to accomplish that makes them so successful.

(2) Clearly, these self-made super-rich appear to be extremely determined. And they're very *persistent* in whatever they pursue; they don't easily give up. They aren't the quitter types. Being as resilient as they are, they are prepared to overcome whatever obstacle comes their way. They know how to deal with crises and setbacks. They possess the mental toughness to hang in there. For them, failure isn't an option. In case of setbacks, they meet these challenges upfront, take action, and move on. They don't wallow in self-pity and become depressed. Furthermore, because they are by nature very determined, when things don't go their way, they know how to wait. These people can be extremely patient. They realize that success will not come overnight. They have a long-time horizon.

(3) In addition, personality wise, many of these people tend be somewhat outgoing. They know how to reach out to people. They have *people skills*. They have realized that starting ventures isn't an activity that can be done alone. They need the help of others. After all, it requires putting talented teams in place to back them up. Moreover, if required, they can be super salesmen in selling their ideas. They have a knack for persuading others to buy into their dreams. And while pursuing their ideas, they will not be deterred by critics and naysayers. Taking no for an answer isn't part of their DNA. If they're told that something can't be done, they believe that it doesn't apply to them. They will always try to find ways to go around the obstacles before them.

(4) Furthermore, many of these people tend to be *non-conformists*. The time and energy other people spend on blending in, these super-rich spend on creating their own path. From childhood onward, they have always been independent thinkers. For them, going

against prevailing opinions has never been a problem. In fact, many of them even enjoy swimming against the current. Some of them might even become uncomfortable when they're under the impression that their way of thinking is too much aligned with the mainstream.

(5) Another notable quality of these super-rich is their sense of *self-efficacy*. They have a can-do attitude to life. They appear quite confident in their skin. They strongly believe in their own abilities, especially in their ability to meet whatever challenge comes their way. They imagine that they themselves—as opposed to external forces—can control their destiny. Being successful comes to be seen as the result of their own efforts. Given their sense of self-confidence, they're convinced that they can solve any problem.

(6) Clearly, these super-rich have a strong work ethic. They're very much *achievement oriented*. They set challenging goals for themselves and others and work hard to achieve them. In whatever they do, they go beyond the call of duty. Given their achievement orientation, they aren't easily satisfied. They're always driven to do better. Whatever they do, it never feels good enough and, if they're not in an achievement mode, they will be dissatisfied.

(7) Furthermore, compared to more run-of-the-mill corporate executives, these super-rich people very much *trust their intuition*. They make many of their decisions on gut feelings as opposed to resorting to detailed analysis. Or to put it differently, they're quite talented in acquiring knowledge without recourse to conscious, analytical reasoning. Instead, they use hunches that surface quickly into their consciousness without them being fully aware of the underlying reasons. Somehow, they're able to bridge the gap between the conscious and unconscious parts of their mind.

(8) In addition, these self-made billionaires will do whatever it takes *to win*. They really thrive on competition. To them, competition is the vehicle to greater success. In fact, many of them appear to have had an early history of competition given past achievements at sport. Sport has taught them how to deal with victories. It also taught them how to assert themselves against their competitors. In addition, it created in them a high tolerance for frustration.

(9) Another key trait of these super-rich is that they know how to take *calculated risks*. They are very good at balancing the risk equation. While being risk-avoidant may have its benefits—decreasing the chance for failure—they strongly believe in the saying "no guts, no glory." To them, being risk averse is not the way to great achievements. At the same time, they're quite aware of the fact that if they were to become an extreme risk taker, they could lose everything. To behave in that manner would be reckless. Instead, as calculated risk takers, they have found a happy medium and have learned to balance these two extremes. Consequently, when making decisions, they will ask themselves each step of the way how they can minimize their losses. They know how to factor in the risk involved in whatever they're doing. In other words, they are risk tolerant but not risk impulsive.

(10) Furthermore, in spite of the opening comments concerning Bezos' glittery yacht, conspicuous consumption isn't what's really important to the super-rich. Most of them do not necessarily bump up their lifestyles in lockstep with their growing wealth. *Wealth acquisition doesn't seem to be their primary motive.* Very few of them work entirely or even mainly for the money. In fact, money is more of a by-product of their way of dealing with the vicissitudes of life. Money is associated with their cherished independence. Money is viewed as a tool that provides them with options and opportunities. In other words, to these people, having more money means having more control over their lives. Furthermore, what should be added is that money is also a way of keeping count of how successful they are. For some of these super-rich, self-worth and net worth seem to be intertwined. Among them are those who become obsessed with comparing themselves to those who are richer. Unfortunately, when this occurs, they can easily fall into the mistake of thinking that money, and not quality time with others, will enrich their lives. Sadly, but clearly, money will not make for a happy life.

In light of the previous discussion, this question arises once again: Do you have what it takes to become a member of this exclusive club?

The Dark Dyad Revisited

But wait, this may not be all that has to be considered if you want to join the super-rich. Perhaps, you should ask yourself what the possession of that much money will do to you? Of course, money can be a force for the good. Conversely, having too much money can have a corrupting influence. It can turn some people into greedy, uncaring, and corrupt individuals. Mammon can be a very dangerous god to worship.

Upon observing how some of these super-rich behave, we might be forced to conclude that a darker part to their personality also exists—something that doesn't immediately meet the eye. After all, wasn't it the writer Honoré de Balzac who said, "Behind every great fortune lies a great crime?" Is there some truth in this statement? Do some of these people have a very dark side? Is it this part of their personality makeup that has enabled them to get to where they are? Is it possible that having too much money may have a negative effect on your personality? Or conversely, was their personality distorted in the first place? What then should you ask yourself if you are one of these people in the thrall of the forces of the "Dark Dyad"—meaning this toxic brew of narcissism and psychopathy (as touched upon in Chapter 3)?

Starting with narcissism, do you, like some of these super-rich, have a sense of superiority over other people? Do you possess a sense of entitlement—believing that you deserve special treatment? Do you think that rules are there for others but not for you? And moving on to psychopathy, do you deceitfully manipulate and exploit people and circumstances for personal gain? Do you feel compelled to win at all costs? Are you vindictive? Do you have a tendency to behave in a callous and uncaring manner toward others—in other words, lacking compassion and empathy?

It could very well be that having these characteristics may be one of the keys to the success of many of these people. Perhaps, the force of the Dark Dyad explains why a person like Bezos puts most of his gains in his own pocket; why he is paying such low wages to his workers; why he appears to be a strike breaker; and why Amazon has been a champion in tax avoidance.[7] There may be some truth in the observation that people like Bezos tend to prioritize profits above profit sharing, personal rights above human rights, and are not interested in the social costs of their enterprises. It makes you wonder, given the nature of their inner theater, whether they are the kinds of people equipped to advance the common good—to build a more just society. Should they be the ones to solve today's global problems? Or should it be the general public? Should we relinquish this task to the more unaccountable super-rich?

If so, what becomes worrisome is that some of these super-rich do fit this Dark Dyad. These people appear to be eager to use their wealth to pursue a self-serving agenda at the expense of the common good. And add to this their tendency to be quite manipulative and greedy at times. What's more, many of them, seem to have a compassion deficit. Many of them engage in self-serving behaviors unrestrained by the usual concerns over the rules or the consequences for others. At the same time, however, their extraordinary wealth gives them a tremendous influence over laws, politics, and public opinion (the latter often through ownership of the media).

Of course, not all these billionaires are prisoners of the forces of this toxic Dark Dyad. If you want to become a member of this club of the super-rich, it is not necessary for you to be an obnoxious narcissist who is manipulative and lacks compassion. You don't need to behave according to the dynamics of the Dark Dyad. In fact, most billionaires are like you and me in that they want to belong, are in search of purpose, and are looking for meaning. In fact, many of them prefer to act responsibly with their money. They're looking for ways to help and to contribute. Some of them may even have had a "Nobel Moment." (Alfred Nobel after reading a premature obituary that condemned him for profiting from the sales of arms bequeathed his fortune to the Nobel Prize institution.) I am referring here to those who don't want to end up being the richest ones in the graveyard.

---

[7] https://www.theguardian.com/business/2019/dec/02/new-study-deems-amazon-worst-for-aggressive-tax-avoidance

Managing Wealth

So, if you think you have what it takes to become part of this exclusive club of the super-rich, there are clearly a few more things that you must keep in mind. If you succeed, will you be able to manage your wealth wisely? As the saying goes, "money isn't everything." Do you know how to make money a force for the good?

To start with, if you manage to become a member to the elite club of these super-rich, you would be well to begin by worrying about the effect of wealth on your children. If you happen to have an introspective bend, you might become concerned that—due to your wealth—your children might be messed up. You might lose sleep fretting that they'll lack the motivation to accomplish anything in life, that they're unable to escape your shadow. You might worry that your children will become trust-fund brats and financially irresponsible people. They might end up with a life of worklessness and be left with a sense of aimlessness and estrangement in this world.

In fact, to give too much money to your children can be quite debilitating. Often, it has been associated with a lack of passion, a lack of creativity, and a lack of drive. Your children may end up plagued by self-doubt about their capabilities. What's more, there is also the danger that your children may display the stereotypical arrogance of privilege by placing a high value on appearances (physical and social)—the obvious examples being the fast cars and the wanton lifestyles. Having too much money may also contribute to an inability to establish meaningful relationships—the fear, and not without reason, that gold diggers will try to lead your children astray.

While keeping these concerns in mind, you may also have realized that you might have sown the seeds that have contributed to the poor behavior of your offspring. After all, it is much easier to pass down money to your children than it is to pass down values. Often, in your pursuit of success, you may have spent long hours at work, while sacrificing time with your family. Now, having become successful, you may be trying to make up materially for your lack of availability during the time when your children were growing up. As you might feel guilty for not having been present, you may now feel compelled to give your children a better childhood than you may have had. Unfortunately, as any child psychologist can tell you, this kind of treatment can be an invitation to much damage. You would do well to realize that the best you can do for your children is to give them a good education and instill the right values. Giving them lots of money is not going to be the answer.

Instead of giving oodles of money to your children, a much better way of dealing with your wealth is to give back to society—to find worthwhile causes. For example, some of the super-rich like Warren Buffett and Bill and Melinda Gates have given away sizable chunks of their wealth. They have even started such initiatives as the "Giving Pledge," a campaign whereby already more than 100 billionaires have pledged to give more than 50 percent of their wealth to philanthropical causes.

In fact, this "Giving Pledge" seems to be a very thoughtful initiative. The question becomes, however, whether it will be enough. After all, how long will the general population tolerate a situation whereby just a few people possess most of the world's wealth? Also, should these few people decide what are worthwhile causes? Such a concentration of wealth is an invitation to social unrest. Therefore, at what point will the population no longer tolerate these income differentials? At what point will they strike back? Wasn't it Aristotle who said, "Poverty is the parent of revolution and crime?" And as we all know, a revolution is no dinner party. On the contrary, most revolutions are very messy. One could go so far as to say that they have a cannibalistic quality. While they may start quietly, eventually they will explode into a barrage of blood, guts, and madness. And when this happens, old things will be broken and swept away—which may include the wealth of the super-rich. So, given what it takes, would you still like to be part of this exclusive club?

Referring to becoming a member of an exclusive club of the super-rich, given the outward behavior of many of them, brings me to the question of charisma. To possess this quality can allow a person to become a force for the good, but as the following chapter will show, it can also bring much misery. Many people cannot handle the chains that come unfettered due to charisma.

8

To Hell with Charisma

> *History is rich with adventurous men, long on charisma, with a highly developed instinct for their own interests, who have pursued personal power—bypassing parliaments and constitutions, distributing favours to their minions, and conflating their own desires with the interests of the community.*
> —*Umberto Eco*

> *The most dangerous leadership myth is that leaders are born…that people simply either have certain charismatic qualities or not. That's nonsense; in fact, the opposite is true. Leaders are made rather than born.*
> —*Warren Bennis*

Introduction

The German sociologist Max Weber defined charisma as a "certain quality of an individual personality, by virtue of which he is set apart from ordinary men and treated as endowed with supernatural, superhuman, or at least specifically exceptional powers or qualities." But is it truly helpful to say that "charisma is the gift from above where a leader knows from inside himself what to do?"[1] Isn't this "gift from above" a somewhat puzzling statement? Does it give a better understanding of the concept of charisma?

What Weber failed to mention, however, is how to deal with the psychodynamics of leader–follower behavior. He didn't mention that human beings are highly impressionable: that when frightened, they look for someone all-powerful—someone who will protect them—which makes them highly susceptible to manipulation. Once under the spell of someone "charismatic," they have no idea how toxic an environment they're in.

Many people labeled charismatic turn out to be nothing more than narcissistic, preoccupied with fantasies of success, power, brilliance, beauty, or whatever else takes their fancy. In other words, they have an exaggerated sense of their own importance and so present themselves as being more capable than they really are. To bolster their self-esteem, many of them need a "fix" of constant, even excessive, admiration. What makes their behavior even more disturbing is their sense of entitlement. Rules are for others, not for them. Many are arrogant, haughty, conceited, boastful, and pretentious, with a tendency to belittle or look down on people they perceive as inferior. They monopolize conversations and are strangers to empathy. They are incapable or unwilling to recognize the needs and feelings of others. All in all, their personality doesn't make for a very attractive "package," which begs the question why, despite this, they attract so many hangers-on.

Unfortunately, there are too many so-called charismatic leaders around. Just a cursory look shows us the very negative effect they have on the world today. While such people may enjoy being labeled charismatic, they seem to have forgotten that they're merely human; their self-importance has gone to their head, and they have turned into narcissistic monsters. More disturbing, however, is that the people they interact with don't recognize their mental flaws. Instead, they enter into a tragic, Faustian pact with them. Bewitched by the demagoguery of their so-called charismatic leaders, they happily drink the Kool-Aid and believe anything they say. Despite their strange behavior, they cling to them, refusing to acknowledge their darker side.

---

[1] Max Weber (1991). *Critical Assessments* (ed. Peter Hamilton). London: Taylor & Francis, p. 98.

The Darker Side of Charisma

It could be argued that many people in the United States are currently suffering from PTTD—Post-traumatic Trump Disorder. Brainwashed as they were over a period of more than four years, they miss their daily dose of the Trumpian idiocies. And sadly enough, Trump isn't the only charismatic snake oil salesman. He is in very good, or rather, bad, company. But is this the kind of company we want to keep? How capable are these leaders? The pandemic has made it clear that when the going gets tough, many of these supposedly charismatic leaders fail to get going. At a time when we needed true leadership, we could all see that these emperors had no clothes on.

Just think how Jair Bolsonaro, the President of Brazil, has turned his country into a train wreck. As the pandemic ravaged the population, with over 21 million cases and over 600,000 deaths by late 2021, he continued to describe the virus as a mere flu that could be cured with arcane, voodoo-like treatments. Consider also Narendra Modi, Prime Minister of India, a specialist in fanning the flames of Muslim vs. Hindu extremism and terrorism but under whose regime the hospitals in India were transformed for a while into a sort of Dante's *Inferno*. Yet, he was continuing to hold political rallies and religious celebrations. As far as the pandemic is concerned, a worse scenario is hard to imagine.

Yet another of these so-called charismatic heroes is Recep Tayyip Erdoğan, the President of Turkey. By locking up journalists who disagree with his utterings, he has created an exceptional echo chamber of sycophants. Anyone standing in his way can expect to be crushed. If he is to be believed, conspiracies are rife. So much for his promise of Turkey being a beacon of democracy in a region riven by religious conflict. So much for turbocharging the Turkish economy. So much for managing the pandemic.

As far as crushing opponents is concerned, pandemic or no pandemic, the military rulers of Myanmar are hard to beat. As mentioned in the introduction to this book of essays, Min Aung Hlaing, the army general who serves as Chairman of the State Administration Council, is notorious for leaving a stink wherever he goes. And he has created a mega stink, given all the dead bodies he is leaving in his wake. Similarly, the president of Belarus, Alexander Lukashenko, is no slouch, either. Both "charismatic" men use torture and murder to deal with dissenters.

However, my all-time favorite among charismatic leaders has always been the Supreme Leader of North Korea, Kim Jong-un. Quite clearly, Kim Jong-un takes after his late father, Kim Jong-il, another charismatic genius. According to his widely dispersed biographical data, Kim Jong-un was a child prodigy: he could drive at the age of three, by which time he was already a very accomplished painter, composer, and participant in yacht races. As an adult he upgraded his precocious talent for shooting guns to firing rockets. Furthermore, like many charismatic leaders before him, he really knows how to deal with dissenters. However, his "re-education camps" are not for the faint of heart.

Presently, of course, we have President Vladimir Putin whose senseless war in the Ukraine has been negatively affecting the whole world. But what better way to rally the "troops" but through a war? As is for all to see—helped by an incessant propaganda machine—this "special military operation" has helped his people forget the ineffective way he has been running his country. And in spite of all the war casualties, many of his citizens remain enthralled by his charisma, as his shirtless, horseback-riding, karate-chopping macho image is to be seen everywhere.

The accomplishments of these charismatic leaders make me wonder whether it is such a great idea to have them around. I don't think it is, especially since the names I have listed here are only the tip of the iceberg. Unfortunately, there are far too many others out there, claiming to make the world a better place while, in fact, trying to make a better place for themselves.

It's been a long time since human beings hovered around fires, fearful of lurking beasts of prey that were trying to turn us into their meal. But surely, as so many millennia have passed since then, we should have reached a higher level of civilization. Unfortunately, civilization is a condition that is apparently only skin-deep. Scratch us, and our original, more primitive nature will soon reappear. It doesn't take much for Homo sapiens to regress. In particular, our basic nature will come to the fore when we are afraid. In such situations, just as frightened children do, we start to look for someone to protect us—to take over. This is how we manage our feelings of helplessness. In other words, in stressful situations, human beings easily let go of their critical faculties and cling to the charismatic leaders willing to guide them. The tragedy here is that in stressful situations, there will always be someone around ready to volunteer for the role, someone who can create the illusion that they're thinking of the good of others rather than themselves, who know how to make the people who look up to them feel special.

Many of these "volunteers" who rise to the challenge are seduced by the sirens of power and authority. According to evolutionary psychologists, the attraction of power has a lot to do with getting hold of scarce resources, of which food and procreation are the most important. No wonder Lord Acton observed that "power corrupts, and absolute power corrupts absolutely."

However, as should be abundantly clear, supporting these "volunteers" willing to take charge is often asking for trouble. This is applicable not only to those under their spell, but also true to the "chosen ones" themselves. They may not realize it, but such "volunteering" isn't always good for their mental health. Basking in the glow of hero-worship might easily throw the psychological state of these volunteers off-balance. In other words, it doesn't take much for the power that comes with the position to go to their head, especially if there are no countervailing forces. In such instances, these newly anointed charismatic leaders will rapidly begin to think that rules are meant for others, not for them, and become entangled in a web of entitlement. Another pattern that may come to the fore is their difficulty in having other people disagree with them. Instead, it is often "Off with their heads!" when people don't like what they're doing and say so. And if that happens, the road to autocracy will be wide open. Enlightened charismatic leaders are as rare as hen's teeth. Given the ambience they create, very few so-called charismatic leaders are able to maintain their sense of reality.

In fact, instead of following these charismatic, larger-than-life leaders, we would be much better off interacting with the more boring ones. Just ask yourself whether you can name the President of the Swiss Confederation—a country that is better known as Switzerland and which, generally speaking, is run in an exemplary way. I'm embarrassed to say that I had to Google to learn that the current president is Ignazio Cassis, a man who, quite apart from his interest in politics, is also a physician specialized in internal medicine and public health. He doesn't appear to be the kind of person who locks people up when they disagree with him. Neither does he seem to be the kind of person who takes his subjects on a wild ride. My curiosity led me to discover that there exists a long list of non-charismatic Presidents of the Swiss Confederation, none of whom, I have to say with great shame, I have ever heard of. But still, Switzerland seems to be run pretty well and is able to manage without large doses of charisma.

Charisma and Transference

As a matter of fact, it doesn't take much to be labeled as charismatic. Often, when a person is placed in a position of power and authority, simply being able to draw breath seems qualification enough to be called charismatic. Something strange seems to happen at the interface between leaders and followers. It is the beginning of the creation of a mysterious bond, a moment in time when power dynamics start to play a role. Power certainly has a magnetic effect: some people are attracted to power while others are attracted to powerful people. The power of transferential processes should never be underestimated.

When we feel helpless, we are tempted to place people in positions of authority on a pedestal and to "idealize" people who seem to be powerful—a legacy of early parent-child relationships. It is the redirection of strong feelings, originally felt in childhood, to a substitute. We "transfer" our fears and fantasies on others—a very effective tool in psychotherapy.[2] Of course, other factors, like possessing a modicum of gravitas can accelerate this process. By gravitas I mean having presence, having some oratorical skills, and having the ability to quickly size up an audience or a situation. Furthermore, it doesn't hurt if such people have the emotional intelligence that enables them to influence others easily. But even people with very little or no gravitas, once in a position of power, will find that other people will project their fantasies onto them and transform them into larger-than-life individuals. And while using the others as a "mirror," many of them have difficulties in containing this process. They start to

---

[2] Charles J. Gelso and Jeffrey Hayes (2007). *Countertransference and the Therapist's Inner Experience: Perils and Possibilities*, Mahwah, NJ; Lawrence Erlbaum; Manfred F. R. Kets de Vries (2021). *The CEO Whisperer: Meditations on Leadership, Life and Change*. London: Palgrave.

believe what others project on them, making them feel larger than life, with hubris just around the corner.

A great example of how a nobody can become labeled as charismatic—how transferential processes can run havoc—is Chauncey Gardiner, the hero of Jerzy Kosiński's novel *Being There*, which was published in 1970 and later filmed (1979).[3] The story goes as follows: a gardener named Chance spends his whole adult life working for a wealthy older man and never ventured beyond his property. When his employer dies, Chance must leave knowing nothing of the world outside the house and garden, apart from what he has seen on the television. He has some random encounters with other people, during which his unworldly, gardening-based observations are interpreted as extraordinarily profound. These "others" influence other "others," and it isn't long before Chance (who has morphed into Chauncey Gardiner) is labeled as a charismatic genius and a potential candidate for the US presidency.

A Lack of Philosopher-Kings

This cautionary tale underlines my main message, which is to be wary of people labeled as charismatic, because it's a sure indication of trouble—something that Max Weber didn't articulate. Unfortunately, Weber never paid attention to the darker side of charisma. He didn't recognize that too many charismatic leaders, like the mythical Icarus, forget their limitations and fly too close to the sun. Very few so-called charismatic leaders are proficient in self-management. They seem to have very little self-understanding. Very few of them reach the Platonic ideal of the philosopher-king.

Plato first described the concept of the philosopher-king in 380 BCE, in his Socratic dialogue *The Republic*. He suggested that until societies were ruled by philosopher-kings, humans "will never have rest from their evils."[4] According to Plato, a philosopher-king is a ruler who possesses a love of wisdom, as well as intelligence, reliability, and a willingness to live a simple life.

---

[3] Jerzy Kosinsky (1999). *Being There*. New York: Grove Press.
[4] C. D. C. Reeve (1988). *Philosopher-Kings: The Argument of Plato's Republic*. Princeton: Princeton University Press.

But is this ideal of an enlightened charismatic leader realistic or attainable? Unfortunately, as we have seen over and over again throughout our history, the road to hell is paved with good intentions. Even the acknowledged role model of the philosopher-king, the Roman Emperor Marcus Aurelius—who, unlike many of his imperial predecessors, reigned with compassion and modesty—fell short of Plato's ideal. During his reign, he oversaw the extensive persecution of Christians and, possibly his greatest failing, supported the right of his megalomaniacal son, Commodus, to rule after him.

Many of these philosophical theories of leadership disintegrate when they collide with reality. In real life, as Niccolò Machiavelli illustrated dramatically in *The Prince*, becoming top dog can be a very dirty game and I doubt whether philosophers would have sufficient psychological sense to recognize it. Plato might not have realized that real-life philosopher-kings could quickly turn into a different type of tyrant, one with an ideological agenda that can be very dangerous. Just think what charismatic leaders like Joseph Stalin or Pol Pot did while trying to force their subjects onto the Procrustean bed of ideology.

In the Dutch language there is an expression: "*Doe maar gewoon dan ben je al gek genoeg,*" which means "Just behave normally, then you're already crazy enough." The not-so-subtle implication is that we should be quite apprehensive of people labeled as charismatic. Even though they might have only an average level of talent, the fantasies that others project onto them will often go to their head. Only very rare people can keep their heads, while all about them are losing theirs, to paraphrase Rudyard Kipling. To be more precise, strong institutional safeguards will be a *sine qua non* to prevent these mental challenges from coming to the fore. For mortal humans, it is too easy to fall into this soup of charisma with disastrous consequences—autocratic rule being the most likely outcome. In comparison, the world is full of non-charismatic leaders who muddle through with reasonable outcomes.

The Importance of Civil Education

To prevent charisma from getting out of hand—to create countries where people keep a modicum of sanity—it should be populated by citizens who are concerned about the dignity of others and a realization that the good of society as a whole needs to be integral to their own private good, such that private and public interests coincide. This requires a degree of moral and intellectual sophistication. But to get there necessitates a robust program of value-oriented education. It implies a need for an educational paradigm shift, implying forward-looking, innovative educational systems.

Presently, many existing school and university systems are stymied by inertia, conservatism, stagnation, and a great resistance to change—the outcome of long periods of neglect. The falling prestige of the teaching profession hasn't helped. In many countries, the best and the brightest are no longer interested in entering the educational field. Clearly, education doesn't offer them the kinds of challenges they are looking for. This situation is overdue for change.

It goes without saying that high-level, basic skills need to be included in whatever educational program is put on the agenda. In addition, an innovative educational curriculum for the younger generation should focus on character development, social and emotional learning, moral reasoning, and other important life skills. Moral literacy will be fundamental to the success of well-functioning, democratic societies. Educators should make their students aware of the moral issues that will affect their choice of leaders—a choice that will influence the kind of life they want to live. Hopefully, by incorporating a learning agenda about civic qualities into educational programs, future citizens will become more engaged with societal issues. They will become astute in assessing leaders. Acquiring a morally attuned mindset will serve as a countervailing force against the decay of moral authority.

To acquire a panoramic view of life, the younger generation needs to become familiar with the interdependencies of the world in which they live. For the well-being of all humanity, this implies accepting the role of custodian of our planet and committing themselves to creating a better place for all. Youngsters need to be shown how personal, local, regional, and global concerns connect with the challenges that face the world today. Such a curriculum design will imply exposing the younger generation to complex ethical dilemmas that will help them to become more sensitive to values, codes of conduct, and moral principles.

Educators need to point out the overlapping and interconnected parts of what it means to be a responsible citizen: independence, inventiveness, curiosity, critical thinking, empathy, honesty, stewardship, cooperation, responsibility, trust, fair process, generosity, courage, freedom, justice, equality, scepticism—and even the importance of moderation. Such a curriculum needs to teach values pertaining to respect for self and others, the meaning of integrity, and the capacity for self-discipline—all with the aim of becoming more civic-minded. It is important that educational leaders make their students more emotionally intelligent since this kind of intelligence is an essential part of character development.

Civic (learning about laws, government, and citizenship), social (learning about social roles and responsibilities), cultural (becoming historically and culturally literate), and moral education (providing the context that guides the rest) are going to be critical elements in such a program. Students need to consider issues of justice, the insidious effects of corruption and greed, and the consequences of excessive materialism.

Clearly, if educators are willing to buy into the credo that "nobody should be left behind," they will do well to embark on such an innovative pedagogical journey. Most likely, making such an educational journey successful will require replacing top-down rote learning with a much more participatory approach. Consultative and collective decision-making needs to become an integral part of such a curriculum.

To create civic engagement, educational leaders should also draw on different kinds of educational technologies: internships, service learning, and community-based activities. The most effective way of learning combines direct instruction, experiential activities, role modeling, group dynamics, psychodynamic-systemic reflection, behavioral reinforcement, and various community-building strategies (class meetings, service learning, cooperative learning, intercultural exchange, social-skills training, and caring interpersonal support). Student participation in multidisciplinary projects that center on complex, real-life civic challenges, which include participating in voluntary service for the country, will also foster the learning process. Again, these various educational approaches promote the development of moral virtues, moral reasoning, and other qualities that contribute to becoming a reflective practitioner—to be able to make socially responsible choices. In sum, exposure to this kind of curriculum will help the younger generation acquire the civic-mindedness and the problem-solving and thinking skills needed to make thoughtful choices in the twenty-first century.

Creating buy-in for such a new educational paradigm will not be an easy ride. There will always be a considerable amount of resistance to change. But if the objective is to create a better society for all—if the aim is to prevent the darker side of leadership from coming to the fore—overcoming these resistances will be well worth the effort. In the absence of such education, to recall Plato's words, there will be "no rest from ills for cities… nor I think for humankind."[5] We would do well to reflect on these words, written so many years ago. And these musings bring me to the conundrum of transformation, a process to be discussed in the following chapter.

---

[5] James Adam (ed.) (2010). *The Republic of Plato, Vol. 1* (Books I-V) (Cambridge Library Collection - Classics) (Ancient Greek Edition) 1st Edition. Cambridge: Cambridge University Press, p. 329.

9

Transformation Challenges

> *If you begin to understand what you are without trying to change it, then what you are undergoes a transformation.*
> —Jiddu Krishnamurti

> *When we quit thinking primarily about ourselves and our own self-preservation, we undergo a truly heroic transformation of consciousness.*
> —Joseph Campbell

> *One can choose to go back toward safety or forward toward growth. Growth must be chosen again and again; fear must be overcome again and again.*
> —Abraham Maslow

Edward was in for a tremendous challenge. As the newly appointed CEO of a large industrial company, the members of the board had made very clear to him that the reason he was hired was to transform this sleepy dinosaur. The company had been lagging in the competition, a fact very much reflected in its dismal share performance.

Thinking about the challenge he was facing, Edward decided to discuss his situation with his old friend, Jack, a senior partner at a premier strategic human resource consultancy firm. After describing his predicament, he asked Jack what he would do if he were in his shoes. Jack then gave him a real earful. The rest of this chapter is devoted to Jack's lengthy advice. He began as follows:

If I were to get involved in a culture transformation effort at your company, the first thing I would do is to read whatever material is available about the organization. I want to have a general idea of how the people there work, how they perceive the company, and how the company is doing compared to others in the same line of business. As you know, the success in changing an organization very much depends on its ability to change faster than its competitors.

Subsequently, what would be important to me is to interview the major power holders in the organization. I would need to have a better understanding of what they're thinking. To get an understanding of their mindset, I would like them to elaborate on questions like:

- Are you dissatisfied with the present status quo?
- Do you think that the senior team has common goals and expectations?
- Do you believe that you have the correct organizational design and processes?
- Does the company possess the right mix of competencies: skills, attitudes, and knowledge?
- Do your performance appraisal and reward systems encourage the kind of behavior that's needed to make the company successful?
- Do you have the right quantity and quality of leadership?

The responses to these questions would help me understand their perception of the organization, the present challenges they're facing, how they look at their company's future, and what role they would like to play in a possibly rejuvenated company. They may also give me some information about the possible elephants in the room—those troubling, underlying issues that remain little discussed, but that can have a massive significance.

Usually, after I have received answers to these questions, I would need some time to reflect on what I have heard. To me, the "incubation" of this information is quite important. Whatever I have learned about the organization should percolate for some time in my mind. Allowing this to happen would put me in a better position to decide whether I could make a real difference. If I think I can, I might be ready to formulate a few hypotheses of the things that need to be done to set an organizational transformation process into motion. I would be thinking of the changes that are needed in the company's strategy, structure, information systems, reward structures, and various other matters.

In any change effort, however, you better accept the fact that you will be facing much resistance. Wasn't it Niccolò Machiavelli who said, "There is nothing more difficult to take in hand, more perilous to conduct, or more uncertain in its success, than to take the lead in the introduction of a new order of things?" The American president Woodrow Wilson seemed to concur when he noted, "If you want to make enemies, try to change something."

Frankly speaking, Jack added, many people are quite resistant to change. From what I have learned, this resistance may have something to do with a fear of the unknown, a concern about losing control, an uneasiness about a possible loss of status and job security, the thought of being personally inconvenienced, a disquietness of not being competent enough to handle the changes, being irritated for not being consulted, and I could go on and on. At the same time, it is fair to say that people don't necessarily resist change. However, they resist being changed. Therefore, whatever the change is going to be, it is important that the people who will be affected become involved in the transformation process.

Given all these different forms of resistance, the most complicated factor would be how to change the mindset of the people who work in your organization. You should know that apart from the various structural and strategic concerns, the real transformation needs to take place within their heads. Change always starts in our thoughts. In fact, going through a change process is like riding this infamous ouroboros, this mythical snake that seems to eat its own tail, gracing the title of this book. If you would like to embark on an organizational transformation process, you might have to go through, what I have called, a **7C** sequence while riding this mythical creature. What I try to say is that you would need to deal with the organization's **Context**. Next, you might need to engage in a **Confrontation** process with the key players concerning the way the organization functions. This step should be followed by a **Clarification** dialogue why the organization is handling various processes in a specific way. Going through these iterations might help the people who would be having this dialogue to **Crystalize**—to internalize—whatever would need to be done. Subsequently, whatever insights you might have obtained, these would need to be **Cascaded** deep down into the organization. Eventually, and hopefully, these changes would be **Consolidated**, and you would arrive at some form of **Continuity** of whatever has been implemented, meaning that the suggested changes have been internalized by all your collaborators (see Fig. 9.1).

Keeping this model of organizational transformation in mind, my interviews with the important powerholders in the company should help me assess what is feasible. It would help me to figure out whether the changes that would be needed could be tackled with the present executives. I would need to find out if they would be prepared to get out of their comfort zone. I would need to know whether the core group of executives in the organization has realized that change will be inevitable. I would need to know how open they would be to change. Cynically, I should add, that nothing tends to happen until the pain of remaining the same outweighs the pain of change. Unfortunately, most often, for change to occur, there would need to be a degree of pain in the system.

Furthermore, as I have discovered too often (to put it bluntly), it's easier to change *people* than to *change* people. Of course, I realize that making this comment sounds rather cynical coming from a person who has been involved in so many change programs and who has even designed degree programs on change management at business schools. However, it would be hard to transform an organization—despite the many structural and strategic measures I might be able to put into place—if the people who work there aren't prepared to change.

9 Transformation Challenges 109

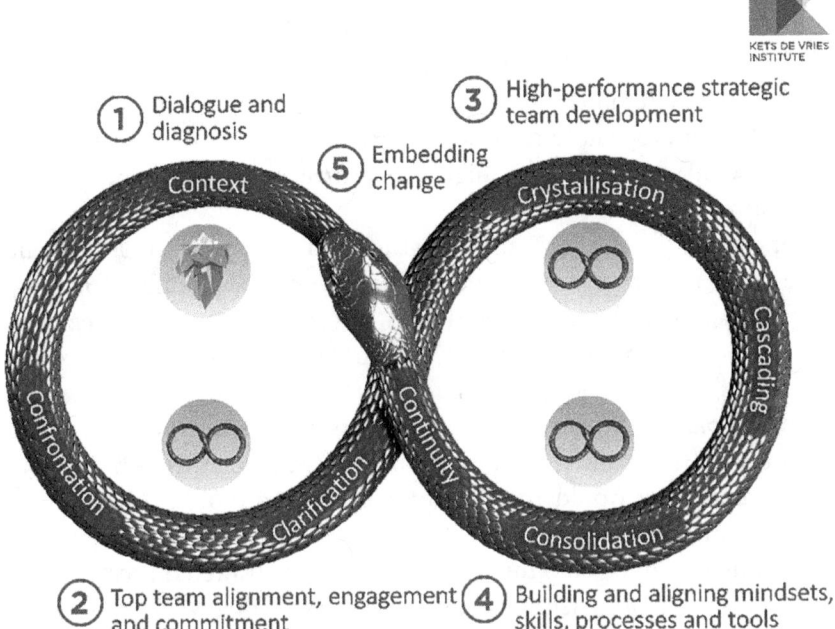

Fig. 9.1 The process of organizational change

A great way to start a change in mindset—something I have tried repeatedly—is to have the senior executives participate in various transformative workshops, starting with the people at the top. Even if you are the CEO, change is not something that you can do all by yourself. Obviously, change is always going to be a team effort. You need to create a dominant coalition that's prepared to stand behind you. You need many others to make the organizational transformation a reality.

Talking about its design, each workshop should be off site. Having such an event at the office is far too distracting. A "playful" ambience to enable brainstorming is better done away from the office. And as far as a time slot is concerned, as I have learned from experience, most senior executives can tolerate being away from the office for two to four days.

I also like to add, again referring to these transformative workshops, that these workshops should not be standalone events. A second follow-up workshop (and, if needed, even more) should be part of the package.

My reason for saying so is that I want to give these workshops some "bite." Therefore, it would be necessary to have the participants go beyond just expressing good intentions. Too many people have made great Christmas-like resolutions, and then have forgotten what they promised to do. Instead, they have regressed to their usual patterns. It would make a follow-up workshop a highly effective way to cement their commitments.

Of course, if there is an agreement to hold these workshops, I would have the expectation that the participants would be willing to open up and talk about real issues; they should be prepared to show a degree of vulnerability. If the senior executives come with a willingness to participate and show some degree of vulnerability, then these workshops would give each participant the opportunity to assess what they're good at and what they're not so good at. It would help them to identify behavior patterns where they would need help for the purpose of creating a more effective organization.

Of course, while going through this process, you should keep reminding yourself that leadership is a team sport. Individually and as a group, the strengths and weaknesses of the participants in the workshop should be discussable. If they would be prepared to engage, however, it would enable them to close "contracts" between each other, to become better at what they are doing individually—and how they could help each other to become more effective as a team.

For expediency's sake, in making these assessments, I have been inclined to use several 360-degree psychometric tests that, over the years, I have been involved in developing. For example, I might ask the participants to complete the *Global Executive Leadership Mirror*, the *Leadership Archetype Questionnaire*, and the *Organizational Culture Audit*.[1] Of course, there are always going to be situations when top executives believe that they are too glorious to complete these instruments. If that's the case, I would have no choice but to interview the people that work with them—a lengthier process.

---

[1] Manfred F. R. Kets de Vries and Caroline Rook (2021). Executive group caching: interventions not for the faint of heart, *Organizational & Social Dynamics*, 21 (1), 134–151 & www.kdvi.com: development tools.

Apart from an assessment of each participant's capabilities and their team effectiveness, the other outcome of such a workshop is to come to some agreement about what the company stands for (mission/vision/values), how the company should look in the future, and how everyone's role can be defined with greater clarity. In fact, these workshops will help each participant to learn "to sing from the same hymn sheet." They need to become more aligned. In many organizations, that's not the case, as I have discovered the hard way. But you can imagine how costly it will be if there is no alignment. To have top management go in all different directions can be a nightmare.

Often organizations suffer from internal "turf wars," with too many "barons" working hard to defend their territory. Thus, an important element of these kinds of workshops is their ability to break the "silos." If that happens, another positive outcome will be that the participants in these workshops are more prepared to engage in real knowledge management—not just paying lip service to that idea. In other words, as people come to have greater trust in the goings-on in the organization—and more of a feeling of safety—most likely, they will be more willing to exchange relevant information. They will become more of a supportive network of people—what can be called, a "boundaryless" organization.

These workshops should be designed utilizing an iterative process; in other words, whatever is done, it must be a co-creative effort of everyone involved. The knowledge obtained through this co-creation process can then be used in the design of the subsequent ones. This approach allows each group of participants to engage actively in problem-solving and therein learn-by-doing. In other words, learning requires action and action requires learning, whereby the crucial piece in this learning process is the built-in reflection process. Learning from the actions that are taken will help the participants to arrive at even more effective actions in the future. Of course, while going through this iterative process, as the leaders of the organization, it's important that they try to paint a better picture of the future. And as described in the Introduction, hope will always be an important building block for future success.

Of course, the ideas developed during these workshops need to be cascaded deep down the organization. Obviously, apart from support from the top, you also need support from the next layers in the organization. Furthermore, while engaging in this process, constant changes in the design of these workshops will need to be made, depending on the outcomes of this co-creative, action-learning process.

I would like to add that having been involved in many of these transformative efforts, if you are able to capture the hearts and minds of fifty to a hundred of the most senior executives in your organization (here, of course, I am referring to very large organizations), your transformative effort will go a long way.

Most likely, helped by these workshops, a buy-in is obtained of what the organization needs to do in the future. This approach, as slow as it may appear at times, is a means to change the mindset of the people in the organization.

Of course, during this process, senior management may have to make hard decisions about some people who no longer fit in the "new" organization. But although you may have to make these "hard" decisions in this cultural transformation program, you should also remind yourself of the importance of building on the old. To completely change a corporate culture may be too much of a challenge. Instead, it is better to work with what you've got and use the best of it.

While busily trying to change people's mindset and getting agreements on the company's future direction, it is likely that structural alterations will need to be made simultaneously. Particularly, the company's reward structure should be in line with what you're trying to accomplish as it will serve as a means of "behavior modification." In other words, if some executives are unwilling to behave according to the new guidelines, you may have to make tough decisions. If people aren't willing to sign up for the new organization, there should be consequences.

Although it may sound oversimplified, that's the way I would generally go about a company transformation. However, while engaging in this change effort, you should keep in mind that when you are dealing with a large "ocean liner," it will take a considerable amount of time to change course. What I have learned from experience is that a serious change process (of course, depending on the size of the company), can take up to four or five years. Some changes, however, can be made quite quickly. If you know what needs to be done with respect to people, structure, and strategy, you shouldn't drag things out. Don't leave your people with too much uncertainty. It only creates anxiety.

Given the fact that culture change may be quite a lengthy process (taking your organization as an example), it's important to create small "wins" during this transition period. These small wins create hope among your collaborators that a better future is attainable. Always keep in mind that each tiny effort will build on the next, so that slowly something great can be accomplished.

Depending on the willingness of the top executives to participate, the kick-off process to have such an intervention should only take a few months. Its speed, however, very much depends on how urgent the present situation is perceived by top management and the members of the board. Of course, in this instance, as you are a new, incoming CEO, presently there will be a considerable amount of anxiety in the company. However, if you use this anxiety in a constructive way, it could speed up the process.

Finally, Alex, I would like to leave you, while you embark on this transformative effort, to reflect on the enigmatic comment of the ancient Chinese philosopher Lao Tzu, "If you don't change direction, you might end up where you are heading."

10

Creating Emotionally Intelligent Organizations

> *All learning has an emotional base.*
> —*Plato*
>
> *Let's not forget that the little emotions are the great captains of our lives, and we obey them without realizing it.*
> —*Vincent van Gogh*

Jack (our consultant from the previous chapter) wondered how to handle another request for help. He had just received a call from an old friend, Rosie, who told him that she had recently joined the board of a large medical appliances company as a non-executive director. Soon after her appointment, she noticed how much the founder Amir—a flamboyant entrepreneur—was obsessed about finding ways to make his manufacturing operations more cost efficient. Slogans were ubiquitous throughout his factories describing to all employees how to solve business problems in a logical, analytical manner. Little attention was given, however, to the role of emotions in organizational life. To Amir, it seemed, cognition was all that mattered. And given the large shadow he cast over the organization, his executives replicated his way of doing things. But in Rosie's eyes it also contributed to a dependency culture, making her wonder how many of Amir's senior executives were truly prepared to challenge his ideas.

Given the way Amir was leading the company, it seemed that, if given the chance, he would prefer to replace his workforce with machines. As he would say repeatedly, machines make fewer mistakes. In fact, Amir's leadership model reminded Jack of the ideas of Frederick Taylor, the father of scientific management, who considered frontline workers as pure efficiency machines. Likewise, the role of each worker in Amir's company was reduced to the repetition of standardized and simplified workflows in accordance to set productivity targets. The power of making decisions was the exclusive preserve of senior management. Very much like Taylor had done before him, Amir treated his workers as pliable robots, rather than individuals with diverse social and emotional needs. To him, it seemed, financial incentives were the only drivers of motivation.

What prevented Amir from addressing the subject of emotional intelligence (EI) was the fact that his "Taylorian" scientific management approach had been extremely successful from a financial perspective. His company was seeing record profits, and as such, it was very difficult to suggest to him that there was something more to organizational life than a purely analytical way of doing things.

To be able to change his mindset, Jack realized that he needed to point out to Amir that emotionally illiterate organizations might do well in certain industries—such as those operating within a very automatized environment with a relatively uneducated workforce. But analytical intelligence alone would be insufficient for jobs that were emotionally more demanding.

Moreover, a closer look at the company's records revealed to Jack that all wasn't well in paradise. Looking beyond the financial numbers, he noticed that the company was experiencing a very high employee turnover rate and notable incidences of stress-induced illnesses. In addition, the fact that the company's culture was "Darwinian" in nature led to a situation whereby everyone was fighting for the attention of Amir. Moreover, the quality of the communication flow between the senior executives and their direct reports also left something to be desired: the figures of a recent work satisfaction study showed that many employees didn't feel safe to speak up in the organization, one reason being that

Amir didn't suffer fools lightly. Errors were severely punished. This fear of making mistakes added to the company's prevailing dependency culture with too many of the decisions being pushed upwards. In addition, from what Jack could see, the personal and professional development challenges of the company's employees weren't taken seriously.

This discrepancy between performance and corporate culture made Jack think of the expression, "nothing kills like success." Too often, he had seen how too much success could lead to hubris, resulting in complacency. And as Jack had already noted, massive changes were in the making related to new markets, products, and possible strategic alliances, raising questions about the company's ability to adapt and to cope. Clearly, it was not the time for senior management to rest on its laurels. The situation made Jack think of Peter Drucker's remark, "The greatest danger in times of turbulence is not the turbulence; it is to act with yesterday's logic."

Jack strongly believed that the people running the company needed to expand their mindset to become EI literate. He thought that such a cultural transformation would make the company agile enough to face what was coming in the future. But getting there, required a shift from a dependency culture to a more team oriented/coaching one. To be more specific, it was high time for people in the organization to engage, have a voice, and become more involved in the decision-making processes. And to get the best out of them, EI would have to play an important role.

To create an emotionally literate organization, Jack decided to discuss with Amir the concerns he had about the company's future, and the important role EI could play to help the company successfully navigate its future challenges. He needed to have Amir recognize the power not only of cognition but also of emotion in the management equation. To try to get his point across, Jack decided to open the discussion with a Zen story he once had heard. Personal experience had taught him how Zen stories, as paradoxical riddles, would often trigger deeper reflection and discovery of alternative perspectives.

The Zen story Jack told was called "a simple cup of tea." In this tale, a famous Zen master was visited by a person who wanted to inquire about the nature of Zen. After sizing up his visitor, the Zen master decided to serve him a cup of tea. He poured his guest's cup full, but then kept on pouring. The visitor watched the overflow until he could no longer restrain himself, saying, "The cup is overfull. No more will go in it!" In response, the Zen master said, "Like this cup, you are so full of your own opinions and speculations. How can I show you Zen unless you first empty your cup?"

The paradoxical nature of this Zen story didn't escape Amir. Somewhat curious, he asked Jack what he should have in his cup of tea. Jack explained to him that he was concerned about the future of the company, given the expected changes in the industry. Subsequently, this discussion of industry developments gave Jack an opportunity to express the idea that changes in the corporate culture were necessary to get the best out of his people.

Jack explained that if Amir were prepared to create an emotionally intelligent organization, it would help his employees acquire a host of interrelated skills such as self-awareness, self-management, social awareness, and relationship management. In other words, Jack noted, if Amir would pay attention to EI, it would make him and his people more self-aware of their strengths and weaknesses. Furthermore, EI also would contribute to the ability of his people to be better at self-management. To be able to control their inner mental states and impulses would ensure that inner resources would be directed to activities where they could be at their best. EI would also enhance their social competencies, so that his employees could better connect with others. And if they were able to do so, it would make them much better listeners; they would be able to hear not only what was being said but also what wasn't said. In turn, "listening with the third ear" would enable them to detect early warning signs of trouble. It could help senior management to do something about the high turnover rate.

Jack had to give credit to Amir. He was the type of person who was always prepared to learn. When asked what needed to be done to make his organization more emotionally intelligent, he told Amir that a great way to start a change in mindset—something that he had done many times—was to have his executives participate in several transformative workshops as described in the previous chapter, starting with his senior team. After all, Jack added, to make change happen is not a solo activity. It is always going to be a team effort. Without having his senior team

10 Creating Emotionally Intelligent Organizations

standing behind him, a culture change would be a pipe dream. Jack also noted, again referring to a possible cultural transformation, that these workshops should not stand alone. As mentioned in the previous chapter, a follow-up workshop should be part of the intervention. It would be necessary to have the participants go beyond merely expressing good intentions. Follow-up workshops were a highly effective way to cement their commitments.

Speaking frankly, Jack told Amir that most people are resistant to change (see Chapter 9). At the same time, he added, it is fair to say that people don't necessarily resist change. They may resist, however, being changed. In other words, whatever the change would be, it was important that the people affected would become involved in the transformative effort. Jack went on to note that, apart from various structural and strategic changes that may have to be made when embarking on such a change process, the real transformation needed to take place within the people's heads. The real challenge would be to change the mindset of the people who were working in the organization.

Jack told Amir that to prepare himself for this intervention, it would be important for him to have several one-to-one interviews with his key people, the ones that would become part of the initial team coaching intervention. He needed to have a better understanding of what they were thinking. Jack explained to Amir that these interviews would help him understand his key people's perception of the organization, the present challenges they thought they were facing, how they looked at their company's future, and what role they would like to play in a possibly rejuvenated company. Moreover, such interviews would give him information about the possible "elephants in the room"—the troubling, underlying issues that prevented them from performing at their best. While further expanding on his ideas, Jack added that it was going to be very hard to transform an organization—despite the many structural and strategic measures that needed to be put into place—if the people who were working there wouldn't be prepared to change.

Continuing his conversation with Amir, Jack noted that leadership should always be looked at as a "team sport," the strengths and weaknesses of each participant in the workshop should be discussable. Therefore, if they were prepared to really engage, they would be able to close "contracts" between each other, for the purpose of becoming better at what they were doing individually—and how they could help each other to become more effective as a team. If so, it would make for a truly high-performance organization. Jack added that, as a means of expediting this kind of intervention, he would be inclined to use a number of the 360-degree psychometric tests referred to in the previous chapter. It was a way of kickstarting the emotional intelligence process.

Jack continued that apart from obtaining greater clarity about each person's role in making the team more effective, the other outcome of such an intervention would be to obtain agreement of what the company really stood for (mission/vision/values), and how the company should look like in the future. As a matter of fact, such an intervention would help each participant to learn "to sing from the same hymn sheet." They would become much better aligned. Jack noted that in many organizations that's not really the case, as he had discovered the hard way. And not being aligned would be a very costly proposition. To have a top management team go in all different directions was a nightmare.

In fact, Jack added, in too many organizations, there tends to be "turf wars." Often, there were too many "barons," zealously protecting their domains. Thus, an important element of such an intervention would be its ability to break these "silos." If that would happen, another positive outcome of such an intervention would be that the participants were more prepared to engage in real knowledge management—not just paying lip service to that idea. In other words, when people had greater trust in the goings-on in the organization—if they had a greater feeling of safety—most likely, they would be more willing to exchange relevant information. They would change into a collaborative network of people—to become what could be called a "boundaryless" organization.

Jack noted that these workshops would be structured in an iterative way and have to be a co-creative effort. In concrete terms, this meant that each group of participants while problem-solving would also be learning by doing, whereby the crucial piece in this learning process would be the built-in reflection activities. Thus, the knowledge obtained during these workshops should be used in the design of the subsequent ones.

Obviously, apart from support from the top, Jack added, to change the corporate culture, Amir would also need the support from the next layers in the organization. The ideas developed during these various workshops needed to be cascaded deep down the organization. It would be the way to obtain a buy-in for what the organization needed to do in the future. But if it was possible to capture the hearts and minds of 50 to a 100 of the most senior executives in the organization, this kind of transformative effort would go a long way.

Naturally, Jack mentioned that while trying to change the people's mindset and getting agreements on the company's future direction, a number of structural alterations might have to be made simultaneously. In particular, the company's reward structure would need to be in line with the prospective culture change effort. Putting the right incentives in place would help the company arrive at some kind of "behavior modification." Of course, this would also mean that if some of the executives were unwilling to behave according to the new guidelines, there would be consequences.

Jack added that although his description may be somewhat oversimplified, that's the way he would generally go about a cultural transformation, making a company more EI literate. But while engaging in this change effort, he told Amir to keep in mind that when dealing with a large "ocean liner" like his organization, it would take a considerable amount of time to change course. Therefore, as such a culture change was going to be quite a lengthy process, it would be important during the transition period to create small "wins." These small wins would create the necessary hope among Amir's people that a better future was attainable.

Eventually, Jack added, if the company would go through such a transformative effort—if the people in the company would understand the importance of EI—an *authentizotic* organization would be created. He noted that the name "authentizotic" was derived from the Greek words *authenteekos* and *zoteekos*.[1] And to be more precise, an organization that

---

[1] Manfred F. R. Kets de Vries (2001). Creating authentizotic organizations: well-functioning individuals in vibrant companies, *Human Relations*, 51 (1), 101–111.

possessed this authentic quality would inspire its employees through the integrity of its vision, mission, values, corporate culture, and structure. Jack continued explaining that the term *zoteekos*—the Greek word meaning "vital to life"—pertained to the question of invigorating his employees—how to help them find a sense of balance and completeness in the workplace. Creating an authentizotic mindset among his people was going to be built on a culture of trust, mutual support, feelings of safety, recognition, and engagement. These kinds of experiences would unite the employees around a common vision and mission and motivate them to engage in meaningful work, having to give their best. Subsequently, their commitment to their work would positively affect performance and profitability. Naturally, these kinds of organizations, being the best places to work, would also be more conducive to people's health and well-being.[2] Jack added that while what he was saying was somewhat idealistic—naturally, no organization was going to have a perfect working environment—it was at least something to strive for.

To give Amir a final push toward creating an authentizotic-like organization, Jack added that without EI, no matter how smart he thought he was, it would be very hard to bring the company to its next level. After all, by not being really conscious of why the people in his organization behaved, thought, and felt the way they did, he couldn't help but live a life full of unwanted surprises. Finally, as Amir was thinking about the possibility of embarking on this kind of transformative effort, Jack wanted to leave him with a comment to reflect on. He offered this one by President John F. Kennedy: "Change is the law of life. And those who look only to the past or present are certain to miss the future." And as this chapter has been trying to demonstrate, there is no magic attached to the process of change. However, the pursuit of "magic" in management brings us into a very different sphere, as the next chapter will show.

---

[2] https://www.glassdoor.com/Award/Best-Places-to-Work-LST_KQ0,19.htm

11

Magic and Management

> *Magic is believing in yourself, if you can do that, you can make anything happen.*
> —Johann Wolfgang von Goethe
>
> *I am a great admirer of mystery and magic. Look at this life—all mystery and magic.*
> —Harry Houdini

People who knew Steve thought he was a little bit strange. He was the CEO of a highly respected company, a whiz kid in data analytics, but at the same time, he was also known to consult horoscopes. Yes, when faced with important business decisions, this CEO would read his horoscope, looking there for auspicious signs. In fact, Steve wouldn't make any important decision without checking the alignment of the stars. When asked why, he simply replied that reading horoscopes was comforting. Though his friends urged him to stop wasting his time on such superstition, his response was always, "Of course, I don't believe in this rubbish, but I still like to take a look. It is entertaining and just harmless fun."

But was it really harmless fun? Despite the fact that Steve downplayed his interest in horoscopes, the truth is that they still very much determined the way he made decisions. And if his decisions came to naught, he would tell himself that it wasn't meant to be—the stars had not been aligned. For him, assigning events to the stars appeared to cushion life's emotional blows.

Historical Musings

To the best of our knowledge, horoscopes have been with us since the dawn of time. There has been evidence of astrological practices more than 25,000 years ago, starting with markers on bones and signs in caves. And these practices seemed to have been widespread. For example, we can find the recorded use of astrology in India since the Vedic period (c. 1500–c. 500 BCE). But it was the ancient Babylonians, Egyptians, and Greeks who systematized astrology. Some 3000 years ago, the Babylonians introduced the notion of the zodiac, an imaginary belt in the heavens made up of twelve constellations pictured in the form of animalistic and human forms. The word "zodiac" originated from the ancient Greek phrase, "*zōidiakòs kýklos*," which meant, "cycle of little animals." In the fourth century BC, this Babylonian star catalog entered Greek astrology, to subsequently circulate widely across other cultures. For instance, astrology was highly regarded in China, in the Islamic world, and in Pre-Columbian Mesoamerica, with astrological practices woven into the Mayan calendar.

The word "astrology" is derived from the Greek word "*asteri*," which means "star." But the word "horoscope" has a Latin influence: "horo" means "hour" and "scope" means "view." In other words, horoscope means "view of the hour." According to astrologers, we should look at a horoscope as a window into one's personal footprint based on the zodiac sign that's assigned to each person. The sign that is assigned to us reflects the position of the sun, moon, stars, and planets during our time of birth. In fact, the idea at the heart of astrology is that the personality and pattern of a person's life corresponds to the planetary constellation at the moment when that person was born. Horoscopes are essentially an astrologer's analysis of the zodiac sign for predictions and advice about various aspects of a person's life, the most common being love life, financial affairs, career, and health.

The Allure of Pseudoscience

The propositions of astrology have never been proven to have any scientific foundation. And yet, according to the Pew Research Center, 29 percent of Americans believe in the validity of astrology.[1] This statistic illustrates the fertile soil in which pseudoscience grows and the human propensity to accept ideas at face value—no matter how illogical.

One of the reasons for astrology's attractiveness is its aura of knowledgeability, given its use of scientific-sounding terms around celestial bodies. In fact, a recent poll by the National Science Foundation showed that more than 40 percent of Americans think astrology is a science—and, by the way, they weren't confusing astrology with astronomy.[2]

On top of that, astrology has become a multibillion-dollar business worldwide.[3] Each day, hundreds of millions of people look to the stars for advice on things like love, health, their choice of profession, finances, and other matters. This interest can be found among all sectors of society, including politicians. Theodore Roosevelt, for example, kept his birth chart on a table in his drawing room. Before making any major decision, Ronald Reagan was known to consult an astrologer. Charles de Gaulle and François Mitterrand also sought advice from astrologers. More recently, Narendra Modi's Hindu Nationalist government seemed to have ignored the recommendations of epidemiologists and public health officials, in favor of astrological advice to open and allow large public gatherings while Covid was rampant. All these people very much followed the Benjamin Franklin credo: "Astrology is one of the most ancient sciences, held in high esteem of old, by the wise and the great. Formerly, no prince would make war or peace, nor any general fight in battle, in short, no important affair was undertaken without first consulting an astrologer."

But not only do politicians ask astrologers for answers, so do business leaders. In fact, in many countries, astrological business consulting has been on the rise, offering advice that is "harmonious with the cosmos,"

---

[1] https://www.pewresearch.org/fact-tank/2018/10/01/new-age-beliefs-common-among-both-religious-and-nonreligious-americans/
[2] https://www.nsf.gov/statistics/seind14/index.cfm/chapter-7/c7h.htm
[3] https://medium.com/@joevennare/how-astrology-infiltrated-the-wellness-industry-945348539a3b

and figuring out the "right energy for a given day" or knowing when "to use the most auspicious timing for strategic decisions." And if these statements are to be believed, for many highly successful executives, astrology has been the secret weapon in their arsenal.

The Need to Manage Uncertainty

Astrology, like all belief systems, helps to ease anxiety about the human condition. In the midst of confusion and uncertainty, we yearn for guidance and support. And astrology provides this illusion of security, predictability, control, and hope in a world that can be otherwise perceived as very chaotic. Especially, in times of crisis, we seek reassurance and something to believe in. The allure of horoscopes is that they help people to deal with the emotional discomfort, as well as the financial, and physical insecurity of day-to-day life.

One way of understanding this wish to create certainty out of uncertainty is to view it as a continuation of the way we deal with childhood experiences. When we were growing up, we were comforted by our caretakers who helped us to make sense and provide clarity about the vicissitudes of life. Astrologers do the same, by providing people with a semblance of certainty in a highly uncertain world. Especially in times of great uncertainty—whether on a global, national, or personal level—people are more prone to regress into such magical thinking.

In addition, what has also contributed to the popularity of astrologers is the explosion of dubious and manipulative (mis)information on social media. Astrology has become ubiquitous on YouTube, Facebook, Instagram, Twitter, and in downloadable workshops, classes, and webinars, offering simple answers within this cornucopia of information overload. Simplification and comfort, however, doesn't mean that we are getting fact-based information.

Singularity and Lack of Specificity

The ability of astrology to enchant is also linked to its bias toward positive thinking. Its predictions are often very comforting, targeting singular issues that are meaningful to people. At the same time, they also lack specificity, making them easily applicable to everyone. Even horoscope writers admit that some of their success rests in not saying too much. Since horoscopes are written in such a vague way, they can pretty much be interpreted to mean whatever we want them to mean. This lack of specificity contributes to what has been called the *Barnum Effect*, named after the famous showman P. T. Barnum, who claimed that his shows, like astrology, "had something for everyone."

Because of its one-size-fits-all approach, horoscopes focus people's attention on the parts of the predictions that are relevant to their own lives. Just consider such typical statements as: "You have a lot of unrealized talent which you have not turned to your advantage", "You tend to be very critical of yourself", "There are occasions when you have serious doubts as to whether you have made the right decision or done the right thing", "You will have some ups and downs financially with nothing going quite to plan." Many of these often ring true to the reader, creating a false sense of validity. Ironically, when we read horoscopes to find out what makes us different and unique, we filter out the fact that they are completely generic.

Human Gullibility

Truth be told, most avid horoscope readers tend to be very gullible. We have a wish to believe and tend to bias our interpretations toward what we desire. Astrology takes advantage of the *confirmation bias*, a process whereby we selectively reinterpret data, searching for, interpreting, favoring, and recalling information in a way that confirms or supports our prior beliefs or values.[4] Hence, in the case of astrology, we laser in on

---

[4] Peter Wason (1960). "On The Failure to Eliminate Hypotheses in a Conceptual Task". *Quarterly Journal of Experimental Psychology*. 12 (3), 129–140.

sections of a horoscope that confirm or support our beliefs while ignoring the rest. In other words, when we can't reconcile scientific data with our own beliefs, we minimize one of them—science—and we escape into mysticism. It explains why people like Steve, who by all other appearances would be rational decision makers, do whatever they can to interpret the text of their horoscopes so that it fits their needs.

Furthermore, what makes astrological predictions believable is that our brains are hard-wired for *pattern recognition* and *sense-making*. We have an adaptive reflex to look for patterns and meanings, as well as irregularities. We like to think that things happen for a reason. Unfortunately, this cognitive ability enables us to imagine correlations when they don't exist. In other words, when two unrelated or random events happen, our mind still tries to see a connection—even when there isn't one.

Other psychological processes at play include a better sense of control, in response to life's challenges, even if this feeling of control is only illusory. Thus, astrology helps us to create an *illusion of control*, providing a sense of stability when we fear that things are going off the rails. Astrologers show us where we fit in, even when it is only based on a zodiac sign. Even hard-nosed businessmen like Steve, who claim that they do not really believe in horoscopes, find that the readings provide them with a sense of balance, boundaries, and order. Helped by astrological frameworks, Steve appears to obtain the certainties that he is craving for.

Psychologists have also noted that more astrologically inclined people possess what has been described as an *external locus of control*, meaning they tend to believe that their successes or failures result from external factors or forces beyond their influence.[5] In other words, they aren't self-determining subjects of their own fate. Hence, they are more willing to have their fate ascribed to them by others. In comparison, people with an internal locus of control perceive themselves to be more the controllers of their own narratives.

---

[5] Julian B. Rotter (1966). "Generalized expectancies for internal versus external control of reinforcement". *Psychological Monographs: General and Applied.* 80 (1): 1–28.

Astrology's Darker Side

People's dependency on horoscopes brings up the question of whether astrology can be dangerous and lead people astray. Should Steve be warned about his reliance on horoscopes for decision-making?

The dangers of the belief in horoscopes should not be underestimated. Despite their relative benignity, for example, occasional pastime readings, horoscopes walk a fine line. In the case of unimportant decisions, using horoscopes for motivation and guidance may not make much of a difference. But can we say the same thing about important decisions? As mentioned previously, a terrible example of the misuse of horoscopes was in India, with astrologers' supposedly "auspicious" timing of mass gatherings during a pandemic.

As this example shows, believing that celestial events intersperse with human lives can have grave consequences. Making important decisions that affect our love life, our finances, our health, and our career based on planetary positions can be quite risky. Astrological predictions or advice can cause people to do things they would otherwise never have done. Sometimes, it can even lead to tragedies like suicides and murders. The fact that people like Adolf Hitler, the ancient Aztecs who engaged in human sacrifices, the Zodiac killer, modern witches, and Satanists have all used astrology for evil purposes reinforces this point.

A More Empowered Way to Go Through Life

A belief in astrology implies a belief in cosmological predestination. It is a form of fictitious determinism. If we imprison ourselves in a fate already written in the stars or other such things (tarot cards, tea leaves, palm reading, crystal balls), we give up the reins of self-determining our own lives.

One of the significant signs of emotional maturity is the ability to make our own choices and trying to control our own life. We shouldn't have to rely on the stars to explain the vicissitudes of our life. Instead, we should decide what we really want and to make concrete, well-considered plans as a way of achieving our goals. If we allow horoscopes to determine our choices, we lose our agency and ability to shape our destiny.

Using horoscopes to make important decisions may also hamper our personal growth, interfering with our ability to make wise decisions. Simply accepting anecdotal stories, hearsay, cherry-picked data is not the way to think and act. In fact, a pseudoscience like astrology poses a concrete threat as it might weaken our critical thinking, limiting our ability to make sound judgments about the challenges we face every day. Furthermore, when we blur the line between science and pseudoscience, it becomes easier to stay ignorant of true science. And as we have seen with the pandemic, the inability to distinguish between hard science and pseudoscience has led to dire consequences.

Of course, for some people looking at horoscopes can be seen as a form of stress management. Given the general positive tone of the predictions, the reading of horoscopes can become a way of feeling better—of boosting some people's self-esteem. For others, it may be a way of having conversations about their feelings that otherwise would have been very hard. It offers these people the opportunity to engage in what would be otherwise difficult conversations. For the more mystically inclined, astrology could be glorifying as it gives them a sense of communion with the cosmos. It brings a bit of magic into what might otherwise be a rather humdrum life.

All in all, some people, helped by horoscopes, imagine that they will be better equipped to deal with the uncertainties of daily life. As a placebo, it may make some people feel better. To have a horoscope provide an answer to life's uncertainties makes these people comfortable. They may even come to believe they have a degree of control because they have taken initiative. It is like having to deal with the uncertainties concerning the weather. While we can't control the weather, isn't it nice to think that through incantations and dances, we are exerting a degree of control? The question remains whether serving as a placebo is sufficient justification for the use of these superstitious practices? Perhaps, we should listen to Voltaire who noted: "Superstition is to religion what astrology is to astronomy, the mad daughter of a wise mother. These daughters have too long dominated the earth." And most probably, he would have agreed with this statement by the American author Edward Abbey: "Who needs astrology. The wise man gets by on fortune cookies."

The idea of fortune cookies brings me to kōans—those paradoxical anecdotes or riddles without a solution used in Zen Buddhism to demonstrate the inadequacy of logical reasoning. These mysterious magical brain benders rely on a different kind of "magic," one that helps people think outside the box, enabling them to disentangle knotty problems. Their so-called magic will be the subject of our next chapter.

12

Kōans as Agents of Change

Old pond frog jumps in—plop.
—*Matsuo Basho*

When you come to a fork in the road, take it.
—*Yogi Berra*

She who eats stones can dance on air.
—*Anon*

Negative Capability

What happens to the holes in a piece of Swiss cheese when the cheese is gone?

When this question was first put to me, I was puzzled. I tried to visualize the situation, a not very satisfying mental exercise. Does this "hole in the cheese enigma" really deserve my attention? Of course, I could be glib, saying something like the cheese defines the hole and once the cheese is gone, so too the holes. After all, I cannot eat the cheese and leave the holes for later. But I also wondered, why would one even bother to ask such a question or struggle with its answer? Was its purpose to jolt me out of my more analytical state of mind?

Since the question troubled me, I put on my logical thinking cap and did some research. Soon I discovered that in Bertolt Brecht's play, *Mother Courage*, one of the protagonists poses this very question. As this play is taking place during the Thirty Years' War, the critical substance of life—during that time—was war. Peace, like the holes in the cheese, served simply as a backdrop to that war—an intermittent occurrence. And, as we know, after a war has destroyed a country, having peace doesn't mean going back to the way things were—just as eating a hunk of Swiss cheese doesn't mean that we get to keep the holes for later. Perhaps in this case, the Swiss cheese metaphor presents us with the image of a situation that can never be restored once it has been destroyed. To further bring home the significance of this strange cheese-and-the-holes question, Brecht's heroine, Mother Courage, loses her son, named "Swiss Cheese," to an execution. In short, he becomes too riddled with holes and becomes irretrievable.

I must admit, however, that despite my efforts to drum-up a variety of logical explanations, this hole-in-the-cheese question has continued to bug me. It forces me to reflect on the less operational matters in life. Its surrealistic, paradoxical nature has helped me to get in touch with my more non-logical side. Managing ambiguity can be hard work.

Ambiguity in Action

Sometime ago, I was observing a meeting taking place at a high-tech company. I had been asked by its major shareholder to help him understand what was going on. A financial consortium that he led had just taken over the company. But he wondered what steps he should take to turn the company around.

After some hesitation, I agreed to attend the meeting. But when I arrived at the venue, I realized that it wasn't going to be an intimate session reserved for the most senior executives. On the contrary, it turned out to be a large gathering, including all the executives of the various divisions. The meeting was introduced by the CEO as some kind of brainstorming session to find new avenues for growth since the company hadn't been doing very well.

I must admit that listening to the presentations and discussions was anything but captivating. The way the meeting proceeded was tedious. Discussions went on and on, with no real closure. These were the kind of discussions that make your mind drift in other directions. Although the various discussants put forth a variety of ideas, in reality, very little of substance was said. Most of the time, it seemed that the different factions in the company were defending their specific interests—often, trying to make a case for more resources. I recognized, however, that their main concerns circled around the ambiguity associated with whether they would still have a job in the future.

Then it happened.

At a particularly low point in the discussion, the major shareholder got up (keep in mind that most people at the meeting didn't know who he was). He then stepped up to the podium and wrote a large zero on the flip chart. Turning back to the audience, he looked directly at them and, without a word, left the auditorium.

A strange intervention indeed. Then pandemonium broke loose.

Many people were talking at the same time, all of them wondering what had happened. But what really bugged them was the identity of this strange person and his motives—Who was he? Why was he there? What was he trying to tell them? A very confusing, but again not very helpful discussion followed. Soon after, the CEO adjourned the meeting.

What Had Happened?

Immediately after the meeting, the CEO came up to me and asked me the question, "What do you think really happened?" Of course, I had given some thought to the zero on the flip chart—and had my own ideas about what it stood for. But what I wasn't sure about was whether I should give an instant response to the CEO's question. I believed that he should give himself some time to think it over. I strongly believed that the incident needed more reflective time. As the shareholder had presented all of us with a puzzle, experience had taught me that in strange situations like this one, the best thing to do is to tolerate its ambiguity for a while, and not to come up with instant answers. I told the CEO to think about the incident—what he thought the major shareholder was telling the audience—and to discuss his thoughts with me the next day.

Of course, not answering isn't always easy. Dealing with ambiguous situations can be stressful. Not only did the CEO put pressure on me to give a response—I also had to deal with the pressure from within: I am referring to my desire to be helpful—to find closure. And true enough, the zero-symbol led to many associations. It made me think of the expression "zero tolerance," implying that a particular type of behavior or activity is no longer tolerated. Was this what the major shareholder was telling the executives? Was he suggesting that they were wasting his time? Did he mean to say that the people present at the meeting needed to change their behavior, otherwise they would be out of the door? The expression "zero hour" also came to mind—that time at which a planned operation was supposed to begin. Perhaps, he was also referring to the notion that the clock was ticking—that time was up. Was he planning to outline a number of steps to "rationalize" the various operations in the company? And of course, there was the zero as a symbol of nothingness, again giving rise to the idea that the meeting, as well as the activities of the people present, was a waste of his time. From all I knew, that could have been the major reason he walked up to the podium to write down the zero. From what I knew about his personality, I was quite sure that he wanted to push the people at the meeting out of their comfort zone—to confuse them—to find new ways of running the company. And his purpose may have been not only to push them into a state of not-knowing but also of hope. Perhaps by acting the way he did, he was hoping to prompt some creativity among them about what kind of future actions were needed in the company.

Opening the Mind Through Not-Knowing

Not-knowing is very difficult. To be able to tolerate not-knowing takes a considerable amount of energy. Most of us like to solve difficult situations. We like to be recognized for knowing. We have a hard time dealing with ambiguity. Even in therapeutic or coaching situations where we are supposed to just ask insightful questions, we will often have our own ideas of how to solve knotty situations. We have this desire to be seen as knowledgeable. Of course, we try to resist that urge, realizing that instead of telling, it is always better to have the other person figure out what needs to be done. Doing so, will make for a greater sense of ownership, thereby improving the chance that some kind of action will be taken.

Moreover, if we are able to tolerate not knowing—if we don't rush to find quick answers—we increase our chances of arriving at a wider range of possibilities. Situations of not-knowing may open a person's mind. An open mind may lead to greater insights about a particular situation. And this will be a two-way street—relevant for both the helping professionals and their clients. If both parties keep on wrestling with whatever problem is presented to them—even though they cannot expect to achieve immediate results—they may end up with more meaningful ways of dealing with it. All in all, letting a problem sink in creates greater receptiveness for different ways of looking at difficult situations.[1] It's what the poet John Keats once described as "negative capability." He imagined that creative thinkers are "capable of being in uncertainties, mysteries, doubts, without any irritable reaching after fact and reason." That was Keats' idea of how to solve brainteasers, his idea of how to obtain greater insight.

As mentioned earlier, the question posed by the CEO of this high-tech company had prompted in me several associations about what was behind the main shareholder's intervention, but I had decided that it would be more helpful if he (and I) spent some time thinking about it. He should pause to reflect on what had happened, as well as listen to the other people at the venue, hearing how they had experienced the meeting. What did they make out of this strange intervention? I was really pushing him to come up with his own interpretations.

The next day when I saw the CEO, he told me, he had decided to change a number of things in the company, actions he realized were highly overdue, but he had been hesitant to take. For too long, he now realized, he had taken the easy way out. Apparently, my suggestion to let him stay with the ambiguity of the situation had helped him, not only to obtain greater insight about the company's present dire financial

---

[1] Robert French (2001). "Negative capability": Managing the confusing uncertainties of change, *Journal of Organizational Change Management*, 14(5), 480–492.

situation, but also drove him to make several badly needed decisions. Subsequently, he was able to persuade the major shareholder of the value of his action plan. The results of this forced reflection ended up being the main reason he was kept in charge of the company. In this instance, negative capability had won the day.

Preventing Early Closure and Allowing for Ambiguity

The ability to know has been an important part of my métier. In many instances, however, in my work as a helping professional, I had to learn to embrace not-knowing. I had to manage ambiguity. I had to accept how helpful it was to tolerate negative capability. But its acceptance hasn't always been easy. As I suggested, not-knowing can be very challenging. And accepting not-knowing is even more difficult. Helping others to embrace not-knowing can be truly an uphill struggle, given people's need to push us—in our roles as coaches and therapists—to come up with quick answers. To resist these pressures can be very difficult.

At present, when I am dealing with an ambiguous situation, the notion of negative capability—the desire to resist closure—always comes to mind. It isn't always possible to adopt this frame of mind, but it is always worth a try. Experience has taught me that by taking this stand—difficult as it can be—I can gain much greater insight. Often, when I'm able to do so, it helps me to find alternative ways of dealing with knotty issues. I have learned that the avoidance of premature closure—to manage ambiguity—becomes a way of challenging myself about some of the basic assumptions I tend to make when faced with difficult problems. If I prevent early closure, that is, if I allow for a degree of uncertainty, I may arrive at far more creative answers, especially when answers are what's needed at the time.

Wrestling with Kōans

To some extent, the situation I have described can be reframed as a kōan—these strange, enigmatic, riddle-like statements presented by Zen masters to their pupils and used as pedagogical tools for training. The Japanese term kōan is the Sino-Japanese reading of the Chinese word *gong'an*, which literally means "public case," since originally the encounter, while occurring privately, came to be cited so often that it became public. By using kōans, the Zen master's aim is to bring their pupils to a direct, intuitive realization of reality without resorting to the use of many words or concepts. And although the use of the kōan exercise as a tool for spiritual enlightenment by Chinese priests was developed in tenth- and eleventh-century China, kōans are still used by modern proponents of Zen Buddhism.

The word "Zen" itself is the Japanese transliteration of *"chan,"* which, in turn, is the Chinese transliteration of the Indian Sanskrit *"dhyana"* or *"sunya,"* meaning emptiness or void. In the *Diamond Sutra*, one of the most historically important texts in the Buddhist faith, there is the famous line: "Out of nothing, the mind comes forth." Grounded in the principles of the *Diamond Sutra*, Zen is sometimes referred to as a practice that involves "thinking about not thinking." The essence of Zen is found in attempting to understand the meaning of life directly—through meditation—without being misled by more logical, analytic thought or language. This is often done through the help of an accomplished teacher. And in presenting kōans, Zen masters attempt to jolt their pupils into making themselves empty, to be open to whatever assignment is given to them. Thus, kōans are seen as an aid to finding out what they are all about. In that respect, having their pupils wrestle with kōans is very much a predecessor of psychoanalysis and other forms of psychodynamic psychotherapy or coaching.[2] Furthermore, kōan practice contains elements of what has been called paradoxical intervention—a complex concept often equated with reverse psychology—psychotherapeutic tactics that

---

[2] Sigmund Freud (1932–1936). New Introductory Lectures on Psycho-Analysis and Other Works, (ed.) James Strachey. *The Standard Edition of the Complete Psychological Works, Volume XXII*, London: The Hogarth Press and the Institute of Psycho-Analysis, 1999.

appear to contradict the goals they are designed to achieve, but, in fact, do not.[3]

Of course, the essence of Zen is the attainment of *satori* (enlightenment), it being the true fulfillment of well-being—the full awakening of the total personality to reality—thereby acquiring more of a three-dimensional view of the world. In that respect, psychoanalysis has a similar objective. As humanist and psychoanalyst Erich Fromm puts it:

> The average person is like the man in Plato's cave, seeing only the shadows and mistaking them for the substance. Once he has recognized this error, he knows only that the shadows are not the substance. But when he becomes enlightened, he has left the cave and its darkness for the light: there he sees the substance and not the shadows. He is awake. As long as he is in the dark, he cannot understand the light…Once he be out of the darkness, he understands the difference between how he saw the world as shadows and how he sees it now, as reality.[4]

What Fromm understood is that the work done by those in the helping professions bears striking similarities to the inner dynamics of struggling with kōans. This is particularly evident in the work of psychoanalysts. Both Eastern and Western practices want to give free play to the creative and constructive qualities that reside within the person. Like the work done by helping professionals, Zen's central aim is to reveal to the practitioner a knowledge of his or her own nature, the achievement of freedom of choice, the search for happiness and love, and the desire to prevent neurotic suffering. In addition, both Eastern and Western practices are concerned about major existential themes such as death, meaning, loneliness, control, human suffering, and alienation. In particular, however, both orientations are committed to actualizing the maxim: "know thyself."

Thus, interestingly enough, Eastern practices turn out to have much more in common with Western rational thought than ever imagined.

---

[3] L. Michael. Ascher (1989). *Therapeutic Paradox*. New York: Guilford Press; G. R. Weeks (1991). *Promoting Change through Paradoxical Therapy* (Rev. ed.). New York: Brunner/Mazel.
[4] Erich Fromm, Richard Martino, and D. T. Suzuki (1960). *Zen Buddhism and Psychoanalysis*. Google Books.

12 Kōans as Agents of Change

Clearly, the aim of both approaches is to prevent people from living without having really lived—to have them reach their full potential. Most importantly, the purpose of both practices is to obtain a greater knowledge about the self—and through knowing the self, arrive at a transformation of the self. In the exchanges between Zen masters and their pupils, which are designed to help them acquire a more three-dimensional view of life, it is kōan practice that becomes the chosen pedagogical tool. Given their ultimate purpose, kōans are anything but random, Dadaist-like utterings; they aren't incomprehensible puzzles. Rather, kōan practice—given the inner journey it entails to cope with ambiguous propositions—enables the person to acquire meaningful insights about the art of living.

To help people in this journey into the self, some kōans are constructed as short stories, while others are presented as jokes, or even dialogues between teacher and student. In addition, kōans can also be depicted in the form of dreams, folk tales, poems, and even as lines from the Bible. Whatever the shape of the kōan, it should be ambiguous; its content should be puzzling. In solving the puzzle offered, however, we should keep in mind that there is no secret decoder ring to help decipher this kind of Zen speak. Instead, its aim is to prepare the mind to entertain an appropriate response at a more intuitive level. The mental effort to solve a kōan is intended to exhaust the normal analytic intellect. But what complicates the process even further is that no amount of interpretation will be able to exhaust a kōan; there is no "definitive" interpretation. To illustrate this point, take the following kōan: Two monks are arguing about a flag. One says, "The flag is moving." The other, "The wind is moving." A third walks by and says, "Not the wind, not the flag; the mind is moving." But like the wind, this narrative is supposed to move you, the reader. It is up to you to decide what interpretation will get you moving.

As mentioned, kōans pose questions that are traditionally non-accessible to the rational mind, but only reachable through the exercise of the more intuitive, creative mind. We can find similarities in much of the work done by psychoanalysts, dynamic psychotherapists, and coaches. Their activities very much overlap with kōan practice in that they both seek to address ambiguous situations. Of course, there are differences.

The original aims of the helping professionals have been to assist people with mental problems, support them in acquiring a greater understanding of how unconscious processes influence conscious behavior and aid them in overcoming neurotic suffering. In contrast, Zen, through the use of kōan, has been a means for acquiring spiritual salvation. But both orientations try to find answers to the reasons for our existence, to find ways to help us to function at our full potential—to help us to give birth to ourselves.

As a pedagogical tool with the capacity to make people feel truly alive, kōan can be second to none. To facilitate kōan practice, the recipient of the kōan will be given what appears at first impression to be a strange observation or even assignment. Its main purpose is to get the person to whom the kōan is addressed out of his or her comfort zone—to look for other ways of dealing with troublesome questions and to arrive at greater insights about the self. After all, without self-knowledge we are like blind people stumbling in the dark. But to be able find our way out of the dark, we have to "wrestle" with these kōans. We need to have their ambiguous content work on us.

I would like to emphasize that, much like dealing with negative capability, wrestling with kōans takes time. This is the reason that kōans are often deliberately presented in such an incomprehensible form. Like therapeutic or coaching interventions, kōan practice will require a process of "working through." The kōan needs to be "digested" in many different ways. Like the Western therapeutic tradition, "working through" describes the complex and extended process of gradual change, including the recognition of dysfunctional behavior patterns, the push to overcome resistances, the impact of insight, and the practicing of new behavior patterns. Thus, working through is how we get from just having new insights to internalize new behavior patterns. Kōans have a similar function. To prepare us for change, they may have a shock effect; they have to get us out of our normal operating mode. That's the reason kōans need to be surprising, surreal, and even overtly contradictory. They have to break the brain's traditional way of reasoning and stop our normal, more logical way of thinking. Like the effort required of working through in psychoanalysis, psychodynamic psychotherapy or coaching, the point of the kōan is to struggle with it—to ponder over the very nature of the riddle.

In addition, we can find an overlap with the work of the helping professionals who employ paradoxical intervention—a kind of "therapeutic judo," whereby a power play is set in motion against the helping professional, which, if successful, has the potential to boost the client's self-esteem, helping him or her to change. Both Eastern and Western orientations to this kind of mind work are meant to give us greater insight into ourselves and the world around us.

Learning, Unlearning, and Relearning

Even though kōans seem to be disguised as "unanswerable" questions, meant to puzzle, and provoke our thinking, some may also have the intention to find some kind of answer, although this answer, at times, may be extremely difficult to find. However, to complicate matters—stimulating this process of working through—there can be many "correct" answers. Of course, the point of the kōan isn't really to find the "right answer." Kōans are never intended to be black-and-white riddles that make for some kind of "Aha" experience. Kōans will always pertain to another form of rationality.

What I am suggesting is that although kōans may seem irrational, there is always a rationale behind them. Strange as they may seem, they have a purpose. They function as admission passes to our unconscious, or put differently, entry tickets to the journey into ourselves. Again, in that respect, there are many similarities with the sometimes-puzzling observations made by coaches and psychotherapists. These helping professionals need to engage in much detective work to figure out the incomprehensible activities of their clients. Like in psychotherapy and coaching, the ability to wrestle with kōans has to do with the capacity to accept the importance of ambiguity in life—to go beyond binary thinking, to get out of our comfort zones, and to learn to transcend constricted ways of looking at things. But while we are wrestling with kōans, we may arrive at crucial insights about our being, as kōan practice leads to greater self-discovery and insight. Kōan practice also prevents us from getting stuck to a particular worldview, reminding us that we do not have all the answers.

Not-knowing, however, can be deeply frustrating. It can even be infuriating. But if we persist and develop our capacity to not-know—this negative capability that's very much a part of kōan practice—the results may surprise us. We may arrive at a much greater understanding of what once may have seemed unsolvable problems. Struggling with kōans—as is so often the case when dealing with clients in a therapeutic or coaching situation—eventually may lead to a greater understanding of the issue at hand. Kōans, frustrating as they may be, can be therapeutic. Therefore, to work on a kōan is to let a kōan work on us. And given the world we live in, we need to accept contradiction and apparent contradiction. Thus, managing the ambiguity provided by kōans will help us better understand symbolic action. Kōans also point out the importance of learning, unlearning, and relearning—how to become less opinionated. In that respect, contrary to what happens in a typical therapeutic situation, the Zen master engages in a form of psychodrama. Sometimes, however, this unexpected approach, the opposite of what seems to be best, is the very thing that helps people crack open the painful shell of limiting thoughts and feelings. Paradoxes can break impasses. The challenge is to release them of fixed opinions and rigid expectations.

For example, when I feel stuck in working with a client, what I have often found helpful is to explore extreme scenarios in order to get unstuck. Sometimes, I also try to apply the kōan method of being counterintuitive—of prescribing the problem as the solution. In such a case, I try a psychodynamic, paradoxical way of getting people to think about their problems. Take, for example, the famous paradoxical injunction, "I want you to be more spontaneous." The explicit message can only be obeyed if it is not obeyed. It is the kind of kōan that's used in psychotherapy. In this instance, I have created a double bind. These kinds of paradoxical interventions can be seen as those in which a therapist or coach seems to advocate for the continuation or even the worsening of problems rather than their elimination. Another idea—also used in kōan practice—is to encourage people to do what they most fear.

Also, very similar to dynamic psychotherapy or psychoanalysis, there will be no endpoint in kōan work. There is going to be a continuing learning process. The willingness to keep on learning is important, as open minds can close all too soon. For example, take a kōan that points to the need for keeping an open mind:

A Zen master who lived as a hermit on a mountain was asked by a monk, "What is the Way?"
"What a fine mountain this is," the master said in reply.
"I am not asking you about the mountain, but about the Way."
"So long as you cannot go beyond the mountain, my son, you cannot reach the Way," replied the master.

Other kōans come across as moral tales, another way of opening closed minds. A well-known example is the story of the two monks, the one being young, the other much older and wiser. During their wanderings, they meet a lovely young woman who wishes to cross a river but is scared to do so. Without any ado, after having listened to the young lady's tale of woe, the older monk picks her up and carries her across. Afterwards, the two monks do not speak again until much later in the evening when they reach their lodging place. At that point, the younger one, no longer able to restrain himself, says: "We monks don't go near females, especially not young and lovely ones. It is dangerous. How could you have done that?" The response of the older monk was: "I left the girl at the river, a long time ago. But it seems that you are still carrying her."

The lesson contained in this kōan is quite obvious. In a way, the older monk is saying that water that is too pure has no fish. He is trying to give the young monk a lesson about what's important for being human.

Let's take another kōan that turns into an important paradoxical lesson in self-management—in a manner very similar to what can happen in Western forms of therapy:

A potential student came before a Zen master and said "Master, I have an ungovernable temper. How can I cure it?"
"You must have something very strange. It sounds quite fascinating. Show me your temper," the Zen master asked.
"Unfortunately, I haven't got it right now, so I can't show it to you," said the student.

"Alright," said the Zen master, "bring it to me when you have it."

"But I can't just bring it to you just when I happen to have it," protested the student. "I'd surely lose it again before I can bring it to you."

"In such a case," said the Zen master, "it must not be your own true nature. If it were, you could show it to me at any time. If it is not part of you, it must come into you from the outside. When you were born you did not have it, and your parents did not give it to you. I suggest that whenever it gets into you, you beat yourself with a stick until the temper can't stand it any longer and runs away. What do you think?"

From a therapeutic point of view, this kōan story is an interesting way to have a person deal with anger management. Again, like a paradoxical intervention, the student in question is asked not to let his impulses govern him but to resort to his reflective self, to help him get control over his temper and not have it the other way around. The kōan showed him how to overcome a serious personality flaw. Thus, although kōans often may come across as strange, even senseless, they are never meaningless. Kōans are mind openers—gateways to other forms of thinking. They help us find solutions to what can be complex human problems.

Getting You, the Reader, More Stuck

As I have suggested, in kōan practice, we cannot apply our usual, more logical mindset. We may come up with what we think is a brilliant response to a human dilemma, but which proves to be without any effect. It's what can make kōans so infuriating. To tolerate not-knowing is difficult. Furthermore, as I mentioned before, working with kōans takes time. Similar to what happens in working with helping professionals, miracles are few and far in between. Before we can expect any kind of change, much mind work needs to occur, coming back to this notion of "working through." We have to deal with the many forms of human resistances that inevitably come to the fore. Also, just as kōans can drive people into knots—so can the observations made by therapists and coaches to their

12 Kōans as Agents of Change

clients. But in both instances, its purpose is to break pre-formed notions and assumptions—to challenge the very basics of our ways of thinking. At the same time, resorting to kōans can help us explore and shed light on many facets of thought that we usually don't deal with in daily life. Thus, working with kōans is a way to open a gate to our consciousness to attain greater insights, inviting us to deeper ways of knowing.

To take as an example another famous kōan: "What's the sound of one hand clapping? How to reach the soundless sound?" Again, this question is meant to short-circuit our logical, more analytical way of thinking—to force us into deep contemplation outside of our normal framework. But what would be the answer? Is there an answer? And if so, is it silence?

Or what can we make of the question, "What was your face before your parents were born?" Again, this question may lead our mind into some kind of cul-de-sac. Most likely, however, the Zen master who asked this strange question doesn't expect an answer pertaining to your face. What's being asked could be much more substantial. It is an invitation for us to enter into another reality. This strange question may get us to ponder who we are—to reflect on our identity. It brings up ideas about our developmental trajectory. Again, we can see how kōans help us deal with major existential issues. While seemingly confusing, they are tools to help us reflect on our life.

To give you, the reader, another taste of kōans, what would you make of the following: "Do you believe that you knew what you thought?" Or, "Why would you believe something that's not true?" And to add to your confusion, "That is not only not right, it's not even wrong." Or what do you think of this question: "Are you unaware of what you forgot?"

It isn't easy to find answers to these questions, is it? Hopefully, I have now contributed to your general state of confusion. But to inject confusion may have been my purpose. As I have said repeatedly, through kōan work, I want you to get out of your normal way of thinking. And as I have mentioned before, pondering on what these questions are all about forces you to enter into another mental state; they force you to pause and enter into the world of reflection. In more than one way, wrestling with kōans is somewhat like looking at a painting, sculpture, or making sense of a poem. And as with art, there is no readily available instruction manual on how to interpret what it is all about. In kōan practice, it will take some time to understand what the questions behind the questions are. But the surprise offered by these puzzling statements are quite similar to the ones offered through art. Making sense of it, however, can turn into a difficult wrestling match.

To present another wrestling match, what would your reaction be, if I asked which color you prefer: green or yellow. But what would your reaction be, if I once more asked you which color you like better, purple or eight? Most likely, you would look at me thinking I must be crazy. Being logical, you might say that eight is not a color. Yet, there might be a moment where you had to pause and consider context. That moment of doubt, where you'd need to stop to think things through, is the driving force behind the kōan. It helps you to value reflection. That's the reason you need to let the kōan work on you; that's the reason you need to wrestle with it.

Kōans invite you to find deeper meanings in whatever is presented—something invaluable when dealing with human dilemmas. They encourage you to be more open to the unpredictability of the mind—to have a greater acceptance of not-knowing. Merely analyzing the kōan for its literal meaning will not lead to deep insights, although it could be said that understanding the context from which kōans emerged can make them somewhat more intelligible.

But let me take another example of why kōan practice can be helpful. Imagine, you're having a job interview and I am the interviewer. I ask you what your ideal organization looks like, and I am listening to your very sensible comments. I ask questions. You answer them. Everything seems to make a lot of sense. Suddenly, in the middle of your comments, I interrupt you. I ask, "What do you think of Marilyn Monroe?" After I pose the question, you may look at me, wondering what you have heard. Was this question really asked? Were you hallucinating?

After asking this question, I recall how some people would look at me, wondering whether I was crazy. Since at first sight I might look quite normal, it becomes confusing. Actually, in situations when I might have asked this question, many people would stop in mid-stride, totally bewildered. They didn't know how to continue the interview. They were stuck. But if you would have had some kōan practice, you might have been able to handle such a question. You would be trained to expect the unexpected. You might even have been able to give a kōan-like answer and been offered the job.

Ending the Circle

As must have become clear by now, the point of a kōan is to go beyond the more logical way of looking at things in order to become familiar with the power of the unexpected. Kōans teach us how to live with ambiguity—to recognize the power of negative capability. They show us the non-dualistic nature of the world and help us to face the limitations of our assumptions related to looking at the world. They show us ways of breaking fixed patterns of thinking. Furthermore, they help us to find answers behind everyday images of reality, to open our perception of the truth, to force us to follow the path of a deeper way of knowing—and being. Most importantly, kōans encourage self-discovery. In being prepared to wrestle with kōans, however, we need to be ready for such a self-reflective process. And to be able to embark on a journey into the self, we may need the assistance of a helping professional. It is not the kind of work that can easily be done alone.

Whatever we decide to do, kōans have always been with us, and always will be. They help us better understand the human condition. They arise naturally in life situations and out of the many dilemmas that we face—and that will come to us in the future. Furthermore, not only does kōan practice prepare us to deal with the unexpected, it also helps us to live more in the moment, as too many people are waiting for life to happen in the midst of life. Kōan practice, like psychotherapy or coaching, will prevent this from happening. It will open us to surprise and nurture that part of the mind where no logical analysis can reach. Kōan practice can be a path to becoming a well-rounded human being.

Let me end this discussion with a kōan, which I have found quite enlightening as it again illustrates that what we think we see is not necessarily what we get. All too often, we see but we don't observe, which is the cause for much human tragedy. This kōan story is called "trading dialogue for lodging" and it is based on the historical fact that if a wandering monk were to make and win an argument about Buddhism with those living at a Zen temple, any such monk will be allowed to remain there. If defeated, however, he has to move on.

In a temple in the northern part of Japan, two brother monks were dwelling together. The elder one was learned, but the younger one was stupid and had but one eye.

A wandering monk came and asked for lodging, properly challenging them to a debate about the sublime teachings.

The elder brother, tired that day from much studying, told the younger one to take his place. "Go and request the dialogue in silence," he cautioned.

So, the young monk and the stranger went to the shrine and sat down.

Shortly afterward, the traveler rose and went to the elder brother and said: "Your young brother is such a wonderful fellow. He defeated me."

"Relate the dialogue to me," said the elder one.

"Well," explained the traveler, "first I held up one finger, representing Buddha, the enlightened one. So, he held up two fingers, signifying Buddha and his teaching. I held up three fingers, representing Buddha, his teaching, and his followers, all living the harmonious life. Then he shook his clenched fist in my face, indicating that all three come from one realization. Thus, he won and so I have no right to remain here." With this, the traveler left.

"Where is that fellow?" asked the younger one, running in to his elder brother.

"I understand you won the debate."

"Won nothing. I'm going to beat him up."

"Tell me the subject of the debate," asked the elder one.

"Well, the minute he saw me, he held up one finger, insulting me by insinuating that I have only one eye. Since he was a stranger, I thought I would be polite to him, so I held up two fingers, congratulating him that he has two eyes. Then the impolite wretch held up three fingers, suggesting that between us we only have three eyes. So, I got mad and started to punch him, but he ran out and that ended it!"

13

Concluding Remarks

There is nothing permanent except change.
—*Heraclitus*

Our passions are the true phoenixes; when the old one is burnt out, a new one rises from its ashes.
—*Johann Wolfgang von Goethe*

The Transformative Self

After the conundrum of kōans, let's turn to the mythological bird, the phoenix. Supposedly, it is a huge bird resembling an eagle but with brilliant scarlet, golden plumage, and a melodious cry. According to legend, it would immolate itself when it was close to dying. From the fire, however, an egg was spawned. And with the warmth of the ashes, this egg would be incubated until it hatched. The bird that was born from this egg would be the same as the one that had died, but it would be wiser and stronger once it reached maturity. Consequently, as many legends and literary representations have pointed out, the phoenix can be seen as the representation of hope, symbolic rebirth, renewal, and progress.

What this phoenix symbolism tells us is that there are occasions when we must die a little inside ourselves to be reborn, to rise again—to become a stronger and wiser version of ourselves. In other words, the myth tells us that suffering contributes to transformation and redemption. Often, we need to burn before we can rise. Whether we remain ashes, however, or turn into a phoenix will be very much up to us. We need to decide whether we are ready for a transition—whether we are up to the challenges that accompany change. But whatever we decide to do, the story of the phoenix can be looked at as an inspiration when dealing with the difficulties that accompany living. It suggests that there can be a silver lining to the hardships that we experience. Each time we face adversity, we may emerge as a stronger and better version of ourselves.

I remember once being in the famous Gemäldegalerie (art gallery) in Berlin admiring Rembrandt's painting of Jacob (I'm here referring to the third patriarch of the Old Testament) wrestling with a mysterious being. Not only is this story one of the richest metaphorical examples found in the Old Testament, but it is also one of the most painted scenes in the history of art. The reason for its popularity seems to be that this mysterious encounter represents a salient moment in Jacob's life. It signifies how he was transformed from a very conflicted, somewhat treacherous individual into a leader. This incident can be read as a turning point. It turned him into the patriarch of the people of Israel.

In the narrative found in Genesis describing Jacob's return to Canaan, he spent the night alone at a riverside bordering his country of birth. It marked the final part of his journey home. However, before entering his homeland, Jacob sent messengers ahead to inform his brother Esau of his return. Clearly, given the dark history between the two of them, he was extremely apprehensive about the encounter that was up and coming. Therefore, he must have been quite distraught when the messengers returned with the news that Esau was coming to meet him but was accompanied by an army of 400 men. Subsequently, in a rather cowardly way, Jacob decided to send the women and children ahead to meet his brother.

While Jacob was pondering what his next step was going to be, he encountered in the darkness a person who would wrestle with him throughout the night. When the sun came up, the stranger said, "Let me go, for the day has broken." To which Jacob replied, "I will not let you go unless you bless me." At that point, the stranger asked him, "What is your name?" His answer was, "Jacob." Then the stranger said, "Your name shall no longer be called Jacob, but Israel, for you have striven with God and with men, and have prevailed."[1]

Whoever was Jacob's wrestling opponent has remained a matter of debate, named variously as a dream figure, a prophetic vision, or an angel. But truth be told, the struggle should be seen in its metaphoric context. Isn't it the case that the things that you're wrestling with could be the things that you've often relegated to darkness? Could it be that Jacob was finally ready to face his darker side? In that respect, Jacob may have been wrestling with his own shadow, the repressed and unattractive sides of his character. And although he may have been wrestling with these aspects of himself in the dark, when the sun was rising, he came to accept that the time had come to really deal with these characteristics of himself. In some way, lying or deceiving others were presented as activities that could not withstand the light of day. Thus, this nightly, courageous struggle of Jacob would be the culmination of his journey toward transformation. It could be seen as his final rite of passage—a turning point. His true self was emerging out of the darkness. Therefore, the journey Jacob had been making—his flight and return to the land of his birth—symbolized his personal-spiritual growth, his individuation process, going from self-preoccupation to turning into God's prophet.

Symbolically, this struggle with the angel also should be seen as representing Jacob's efforts to decide who he would really like to be. It signified a kind of identity crisis, being torn between his own uncontrollable desires—manifested in a life guided by deception for gain—and the final acceptance of his life's true purpose. It explained why, as the sun was rising, he adopted a new name—the name of Israel, meaning "he who wrestles with God." This new name reflected not only his own personal struggle but also a foreboding of the destiny of an entire people.

Jacob had moved toward a state of authenticity and sincerity, qualities that would bring him within the spirit of God. His transformed state of mind lifted him up to patriarchal status. This time, through will and

---

[1] https://en.wikipedia.org/wiki/Masoretic_Text

determination, Jacob had been able to obtain a blessing from his opponent, undoing the deceptive blessing he once received from his own father. After all, in his previous life, Jacob had used whatever qualities he possessed as a means of trying to obtain legitimacy through deception. Now, he had attained a stage of genuine transformation, quite much different from the pseudo-transformation that he had gained before through using guile. He had acquired the strengths of character to face adversity squarely; to confront whatever difficulties that would come his way in a forthright manner. That's what transformed Jacob into one of the great patriarchs to be found in the Old Testament.

Like the phoenix, Jacob had been reborn. He was now strong enough to face the shadow side of himself. He had managed to reinvent himself, becoming a more rounded, thoughtful human being. Thus, although at first glance, Jacob's struggle with this mysterious being comes across as abrupt and vague, it should also be seen as a metaphor for the human condition. This ancient story helps us to shed light on the darker forces that we all must struggle with—how we all search for life's meaning.

We need to remind ourselves that before Jacob became a foundational figure, he was anything but a leader of men. On the contrary, he had been much more of a trickster. According to the biblical story, he had been subjected to the forces of envy, jealousy, power, greed, and lust. He had been quite an unattractive role model. Of course, taking a psychodynamic-systemic lens, we can find explanations for why he behaved the way he did. The fact that he was born second would have very much played a role. Most likely, it contributed to his unstable sense of identity, to his insecure self-image. In fact, for the greater part of his life, Jacob's personality had been colored by his rivalry with his well-defined sibling, Esau. At the top of his mind there had always been his desire to find ways to usurp his brother's position—to move into the place of primogenitor. Probably in doing so, he might have been manipulated by his mother Rebecca. Eventually, by turning into an impostor, Jacob was able to steal his father's blessings, boons that were meant for his brother Esau. Subsequently, after having understood what had happened, Esau had vowed to kill him. No wonder that Jacob had been running for his life. However, this flight from Canaan should be seen as the first step toward his individuation process. It would be the beginning of a process of transformation. During his journey in the wilderness, being cut off from the known world of family and community, anxious and confused, Jacob was trying to find his way.

In fact, after his deception and while traveling through the desert fleeing from his brother Esau, Jacob stopped for the night to rest. That night he had the frightening dream of a ladder or staircase reaching into heaven with angels wandering up and down it, commonly referred to as "Jacob's ladder"—another scene painted by many artists. One way of interpreting this strange dream of Jacob's ladder is to view it as being symbolic of the connection between heaven and earth, representing progress, ascension, and a spiritual passage through various levels of initiation. In other words, Jacob's ladder could be read as a sign of Jacob's upcoming transformation—his possible transition into a new state of consciousness. The dream may have signified that his role as a trickster was ending. Whatever he would accomplish in the future, this time it would happen through his own efforts. But before he would be capable of doing so, he had to pass many tests. Further challenges would be awaiting him. According to the biblical tale, for many decades, he would be slaving for Laban, his father-in-law. But these years away from his country of birth prepared him for his personal transformation—his ability to reinvent himself.

Creative Destruction

Like the story of Jacob, this book of essays is symbolic of rebirth and renewal. It explains why I used as markers the ouroboros and phoenix in the beginning and the end. Creation, resurrection, hope, and new beginnings are the recurrent themes associated with these two mythical creatures. Like the ouroboros, the phoenix also brings up associations of self-improvement, reinvention, and transformation. Also, these mythical creatures symbolize the ability to grow through adversity, to re-emerge. These dynamics can be looked at as the red threads that go through the various essays of this book. They are reminders of our ability to reinvent ourselves—to become what we can be. They help us reframe setbacks as opportunities for growth and development. Hence, despite the negative associations we may have had reading the various essays, whatever is presented also serves as reminders that life can be different if the protagonists in these stories would have been able to reframe the way they looked at the world. Thus, though the essays in this book often describe the negativity of the human condition, they also, at the same time, suggest ways of transcending this negativity—to go beyond destructiveness.

In the essays in this book, life would have become so much better if the protagonists would have been able to divert themselves from their mental models—if they could look at life with greater positivity. Instead, all too often, they seemed to be hanging on to mental models that no longer were appropriate. Their *Weltanschauung* had become self-reinforcing, self-sustaining, and self-limiting, often with catastrophic effects. And predictably, when mental models are no longer in sync with reality, it will be a prescription for disaster.

Clearly, many of the protagonists in these essays appeared to be stuck. They didn't realize that every act of creation would also be an act of destruction. After all, the creation of something new and different—something that has not yet been done—demands the destruction of the old. In fact, the presence of destruction is at the core of the creative process itself. No wonder that the ouroboros and phoenix symbolism can be so powerful, as it is suggestive of renewal. Therefore, my hope is that the readers of these essays will do the same—that they will be inspired to look for ways of personal reinvention, ways to embrace the process of creative destruction.

Furthermore, as has become clear from these essays, too many people live within unhappy circumstances. Stuck in their comfort zone, they are addicted to a life of security and conformity. But these are the conditions that kill the adventurous spirit, which takes the nerve out of them. Unfortunately, such people haven't realized that life begins at the end of their own comfort zone. They may not be aware of the fact that they have reached a point in their lives when change is required—that they need to make a fresh start—that it is high time to reinvent themselves and strive for a new purpose, goal, or dream.

Sadly enough, many people become more aware of this need for reinvention when things are very bad. Only when times have gotten truly tough do they experience the need to refocus—to become resourceful. Only then, like the phoenix, do they come to realize that they must die inside if they are to rise from their own ashes and become a new person. But despite all the hardships, just as in the case of the biblical Jacob, they could also look at adversity as an opportunity to rebuild themselves in the way they would have liked to have been all along. Or to quote Friedrich Nietzsche once more: "One must have chaos in oneself to be able to give birth to a dancing star."[2]

I hope the reader realizes that when we're tired of the ways things are and want to spark change in our lives, then the time has arrived to really embrace being our authentic and true self. It should be looked at as a moment in time, when we should be prepared to re-examine the stories we've been telling about ourselves—what we think we're all about. After all, it will be very difficult to change, unless we're aware of what needs to be changed. And as has been the case of Jacob, through a reflective struggle, we may discover that what we used to believe no longer seems to apply to our present-day reality. On the contrary, it has blocked us from growing and reaching our goals. This will be the moment in time when we should identify our negative or limiting beliefs, to take true responsibility for our life choices. At the same time, we should also not forget to use our past experiences as lessons and not as obstacles when entering our new phase in life. It is only through the re-framing and letting go of self-limiting concepts that we will be capable to continue the important journey of becoming our true, authentic selves. Getting there can be quite a wild ride. However, quoting Lao Tzu once more, "When I let go of what I am, I become what I might be."

---

[2] Friedrich Nietzsche (1883/1978), *Thus Spoke Zarathustra*, New York: Vintage Books, p. 17.

Index[1]

A
Abbey, Edward, 131
Acton, John Dalberg-Acton, 1st Baron, 8, 97
Adam and Eve, 56
Addiction, 57
Aesop, 41
Agreeableness, 84
Aha experiences, 9, 143
Alcohol, 15, 27, 62
Altruism, 38
Amazon, 16, 89
Anger, 16–18, 28, 34, 36, 57, 63, 71
Anger management, 146
Anxiety, 9, 15, 18, 66, 71, 72, 75, 76, 78, 113, 126
Aquinas, Thomas, 13
Arendt, Hannah, 24, 25
Aristotle, 92
Asceticism, 14
al-Assad, Bashar, 30
Assault, 27, 29, 45, 50
Astrology
  dark side, 129
  gullibility and, 127–128
  singularity, 127
  specificity lack of, 127
  uncertainty and, 126, 130
Astronomy, 125, 131
Atrocities, 23–26, 29–31
Atropos, 12
Attention-deficit/hyperactivity disorder (ADHD), 71
Authenticity, 4, 7, 153
Autocracy, 97
Aztec civilization, 129

---

[1] Note: Page numbers followed by 'n' refer to notes.

Index

B

Babylon, ancient, 124
Banality of evil, 24
Barnum, Phineas Taylor, 127
Barons, 53, 111, 120
Behavioral mimicry, 32
Behavior modification, 112, 121
Being There (Kosiński), 99
Belarus, 8, 30, 96
Belfort, Jordan, 22
Bennis, Warren, 93
Berra, Lawrence Peter 'Yogi,' 133
Bezos, Jeffrey, 16, 81, 82, 88–90
Bhopal disaster (1984), 43
Big Five model, 84
Big Quit, 18
Billionaires, *see* Super-rich people
Bolsonaro, Jair, 8, 95
Botticelli, Sandro, 14
Boundaryless organization, 111, 120
Brain
   mirror neurons, 33
   psychopathy and, 28, 28n3, 35, 48–49, 89
   violence and, 17
Brazil, 8, 95
Brecht, Bertolt, 134
Bribery, 42
Bruegel the Elder, Peter, 13
Buddhism, 149
Buffett, Warren, 83, 92

C

Campbell, Joseph, 2
Camus, Albert, 21
Capability, 46, 49, 91, 111, 133–134, 137, 138, 142, 144, 149
Carnegie, Andrew, 82
Cassis, Ignazio, 97
Chanel, Gabrielle 'Coco,' 81
Character armor, 5–6
Charisma
   civil education and, 101–103
   definition of, 93
   narcissism and, 28, 28n3, 89
   philosopher-kings, 99, 100
   transference and, 98–99
Charity, 20
Chastity, 20
China, 82, 124, 139
China Sanlu milk scandal (2008), 43
Christianity seven deadly sins, 10, 13–20
Cicero, 12
Civil education, 101–103
Clotho, 12
Commodus, Roman Emperor, 100
Compassion, 7, 28, 30, 35, 38, 64, 89, 90, 100
Confirmation bias, 127
Confucius, 31
Conscientiousness, 72, 84
Control, illusion of, 128
Control systems, 52
Cooperation, 102
Copyright infringement, 42
Corporate bribery, 23
Corporate culture, 44, 51, 112, 117, 118, 121, 122
Corporate psychopathy, 48–49
Corporate violence, 23
Courage, 3, 12, 34, 102
Covid-19 pandemic
   female leaders and, 20
   seven deadly sins and, 10, 13–20
   vaccines, 16

Creative accounting, 51
Creative destruction, 155–157
Crime white-collar, 10, 41–54
Critical thinking, 102, 130
Curie, Marie, 12
Curiosity, 77, 98, 102
Cybercrime, 22, 42
Cyberloafing, 17

D

Dadaism, 141
Dante Alighieri, 14, 95
Dark dyad, 28, 89–90
de Balzac, Honoré, 89
De Gaulle, Charles, 125
Dehumanization, 36
Delphi, Greece, 9
Demagoguery, 94
Dependency culture, 115, 117
Depression, 2, 9, 57, 69, 72
Desert fathers, 14
Diamond Sutra, 139
Diesel dupe scandal (2015), 43
Diligence, 20, 50, 52
Divine Comedy, The (Dante), 14
Dostoyevsky, Fyodor, 12
Drucker, Peter, 117
Drugs, 27, 47, 62

E

Eating disorders, 57
Eco, Umberto, 93
Education, 35, 42, 53, 92, 101–103
Egypt, ancient, 1, 2
Eichmann, Adolf, 24, 25, 36
Einstein, Albert, 25
Embezzlement, 42, 45
Emotional contagion, 33
Emotional imprinting, 59
Emotional intelligence (EI), 98, 116–118, 120–122
   authentizotic organization, 121
Empathy, 7, 28, 35, 38, 48, 49, 89, 94, 102
Entrepreneurship, 85
Entry and exit, 52
Envy, 13, 14, 18, 20, 28, 34, 154
Equality, 102
Erdoğan, Recep Tayyip, 95
Erikson, Erik, 2
Ethical standards, 52
Evagrius the Solitary, 14
Evil
   drugs and, 27
   enterprises, 23
   group dynamics and, 25
   idealistic fanaticism and, 22
   as means to an end, 22
   mental acrobatics and, 30
   non-action and, 25
   nurture and nature, 28–29
   obedience to authority, 24–25
   parenting and, 33–36
   personality and, 28
   personal responsibility and, 35, 36
   prevention of, 31
   rationalization of, 30
   self-esteem and, 22
   selfish gene theory, 29
Evil Corp, 21
External locus of control, 128
Extraversion, 84

F

Fair process, 102
Fates, 11–12, 128, 129
Female leaders, 20
Fight or flight response, 49
Financial Times, 42
First, do no harm, 31
Fitzgerald, Francis Scott, 83
Forbes, 82
Ford, Henry, 82
Forgery, 42
Franklin, Benjamin, 125
Fraud, 42–46, 50, 52
Fraud Diamond, 46
Fraud Triangle, 44–46, 50
Freedom, 85, 102, 140
French, Robert, 22, 137n1
Freud, Sigmund, 7
Fromm, Erich, 140
Frustration, 3, 17, 18, 34, 87

G

Gallup, 43
Gandhi, Mohandas, 39
Gates, Melinda, 92
Gates, William 'Bill,' 83
Gattopardo Il (Tomasi di Lampedusa), 11
Gemäldegalerie, Berlin, 152
Generosity, 102
Genocide, 23, 25, 29
Giving Pledge, 92
Global Executive Leadership Mirror, 110
Global financial crisis (2008), 43
Gluttony, 13–15, 20
Great Resignation, 18
Greece, ancient, 11, 69, 124
Greed, 9, 13, 14, 16, 20, 46–47, 54, 102, 154
Greensill, Alexander 'Lex,' 41
Gregory I, Pope, 13
Grief, 18
Group dynamics, 25–27, 38, 103
Guilt, 17, 34, 45, 48, 57, 58, 69
Gupta, Sanjeev, 41, 42

H

Hedonic treadmill, 46
Heraclitus, 151
Hermits, 14, 145
Hippocrates, 31
Hitler, Adolf, 35, 129
Holocaust, 24, 25
Honesty, 43, 102
Hope, 3, 9, 10, 12, 13, 23, 36, 68, 111, 113, 121, 126, 136, 151, 155–157
Horoscopes, 123, 124, 126–130
Houdini, Harry, 123
Hubris, 7, 19, 99, 117
Human sacrifices, 129
Humility, 7, 20
Hyper-masculinity, 19

I

Icarus, 99
Identity theft, 42
Illusion of control, 128
Imitation, 32, 99, 149
Imprinting, 59
Incrementalism, 4
Incubation process, 5
Independence, 85, 88, 102
India, 43, 95, 124, 129

Inferno (Dante), 14, 95
Infinity, 2
Inner demons, 4, 9
Insider trading, 42
Insurance, 45
Integrity-versus-despair, 2
Interdependencies, 102
Inventiveness, 102

Jacob, 152–155, 157
James, William, 3, 79, 103n5
Jobs, Steve, 83
Jung, Carl, 24, 36, 56
Justice, 102

Kalanick, Travis, 83
Keats, John, 137
Kennedy, John Fitzgerald, 122
Kim Jong-un, 96
Kindness, 20, 35, 38, 77
Kipling, Rudyard, 100
Know thyself maxim, 140
Kōans, 11, 131, 133–151
   counterintuitiveness, 144
   etymology of, 139
   not knowing, 11, 144, 146, 148
   wrestling with, 139–143, 147
Kosiński, Jerzy, 99
Krishnamurti, Jiddu, 105

Lachesis, 12
Lao Tzu, 113, 157
Laziness, 17

Leadership Archetype Questionnaire, 110
Leadership development programs, 51
Lukashenko, Alexander, 8, 30, 96
Lust, 13–15, 20, 154

Ma, Jack, 83
Machiavelli, Niccolò, 100, 107
Macro level perspective, 7
Madoff, Bernard, 22, 42, 45, 46, 50
Magic, 11, 122–131
Mandela, Nelson, 9
Marcus Aurelius, Roman Emperor, 100
Maslow, Abraham, 105
Mass shootings, 23
Matsuo Basho, 133
Mayan civilization, 124
Mental acrobatics, 30, 57
Micro-level perspective, 7
Milgram, Stanley, 26, 26n2, 27
Min Aung Hlaing, 8, 30, 95
Mirror neurons, 33
Mitterrand, François, 125
Mob violence, 23
Moderation, 102
Modi, Narendra, 95, 125
Moirai, 11, 12
Money-laundering, 42
Moral development, 32–34
Morality, 30, 31
Morgan, John Pierepont, 82
Mother Courage (Brecht), 134
Mugabe, Robert, 8
Murder, 27, 29–31, 50, 96, 129
Musk, Elon, 16, 83
Myanmar, 8, 30, 95

N

Narcissism, 28, 28n3, 89
National Science Foundation, 125
Near-death experiences, 3, 6
Negative capability, 133–134, 137, 138, 144, 149
Neuroticism, 84
Nietzsche, Friedrich, 5, 157
Nin, Anaïs, 55
Nobel, Alfred, 90
Non-action, 25
North Korea, 96
Not-knowing, 11, 136–138, 144, 146, 148

O

Obedience to authority, 24–26, 35, 38
Obsessive-compulsive disorder (OCD), 71
Once-borns, 3, 6
Openness to experience, 84
Opportunity, 2, 15, 16, 19, 21–39, 44, 47, 48, 51, 52, 82, 88, 110, 118, 130, 155, 157
Organizational Culture Audit, 110
Ouroboros
  etymology of, 1–2
  phoenix comparison, 11

P

Paleolithic period, 29, 58
Paranoia, 9
Parenting
  evil and, 33–36
  shame and, 59
Pascal, Blaise, 22
Passive-aggressive behavior, 71

Patience, 20
Pattern recognition, 128
Peak experience, 6
Perfect crime, 52–54
Perfection, 3, 75, 76
Perfectionism, 57, 71, 75–76, 78
Personality
  evil and, 24, 27
  plasticity of, 60
  shame and, 60
Pew Research Center, 125
Philosopher-kings, 99–100
Phoenix, 151, 152, 154–156
Piaget, Jean, 32n4
Plato, 99, 100, 103, 140
Pollution, 23
Pol Pot, 100
Ponzi schemes, 22, 42, 50
Populism, 9, 37
Positive thinking, 127
Practical jokes, 26
Pressure, 15, 22, 44, 46, 47, 67, 71, 136, 138
Price-fixing, 45
Pride, 13, 14, 18–20
Prince, The (Machiavelli), 100
Procrastination
  behavioural recommendations, 72–75
  busyness and, 74
  character types and, 71–72
  control, 71
  etymology of, 69
  evolutionary perspective, 70
  fun and, 75
  perfectionism and, 75–76
  pressure and, 71
  rebelliousness and, 71
  self-control and, 73
  self-forgiveness and, 77

superego and, 77–79
test, 68–69
time management, 74
too big a task, 73
Projection, 15
Prudentius, Aurelius Clemens, 20
Pseudoscience, 125–126, 130
Psychomachia (Prudentius), 20
Psychometric tests, 110, 120
Psychopathy, 28, 28n3, 35, 48–49, 89
Punishment of errors, 117
Purgatory, 4, 5

R

Ransomware, 22, 28
Rapists, 28
Rationalization, 30, 44, 45
Reagan, Ronald, 125
Rebirth, 1–3, 6, 151, 155
Red thread, 6–11, 155
Reframing, 65, 72, 73
Regression, 31
Relationship management, 118
Religion, 23, 42, 130
Rembrandt van Rijn, 152
Republic, The (Plato), 99
Responsibility, 12, 14, 17, 31, 35–37, 44, 45, 53, 72, 102, 157
Revolutions, 92
Risk-taking, 47
Rockefeller, John, 82
Roosevelt, Theodore, 125
Russia, 82

S

Sanlu milk scandal (2008), 43
Satanists, 129
Satori, 140

Scepticism, 102
Schiller, Friedrich, 41
School bullies, 28
Secure base, 32–36
Self-actualization, 4
Self-awareness, 34
Self-compassion, 64, 72, 75–78
Self-confidence, 28, 32, 76, 87
Self-control, 20, 27, 47, 70, 73
Self-esteem, 22, 59, 65, 94, 130, 143
Self-forgiveness, 77
Selfish gene theory, 29
Self-management, 118
Self-sabotage, 79
Seneca, 67
Sense-making, 128
Serial killers, 28
7C sequence, 108
Seven deadly sins, 10, 13–20
Sex, 14, 15, 22
Sexual abuse, 23
Shakespeare, William, 13
Shamanism, 7
Shame
    acknowledgement of, 61
    etymology of, 56
    evolutionary perspective, 58
    guilt, comparison with, 30, 34, 56, 58, 69
    master emotion, 66
    origins, looking for, 66
    overcoming, 60–62, 64
    physiological responses, 56
    professional help, 65
    psychological perspective, 59
    recognizing the signs, 63
    self-forgiveness and, 58
    sharing the problem, 61

Silos, 111, 120
Simple cup of tea story, 117
Singing from hymn sheet, 111, 120
Sloth, 13, 14, 17, 20
Social awareness, 118
Social media, 17, 37, 126
Solzhenitsyn, Aleksander, 23
Stalin, Joseph, 35, 100
Stanford prison experiment (1971), 26n2
Stewardship, 102
Suicide, 50, 57, 129
Suicide bombers, 23, 29
Summer camps, 26
Superego, 77–79
Super-rich people
    achievement orientation, 87
    Big Five model and, 84
    big ideas and, 86
    calculated risks, 88
    children of, 91, 92
    competitiveness and, 87
    control and, 85, 88
    dark dyad and, 89, 90
    entrepreneurship and, 85
    giving back, 92
    intuition and, 87
    magnificent obsession, 86
    money, importance of, 85, 88–92
    non-conformity, 86
    people skills, 86
    persistence, 86
    self-efficacy, 87
Sutherland, Edwin, 42
Swiss cheese, 133, 134
Switzerland, 97, 98

T

Taylor, Frederick, 116
Temperance, 20
Temple of Apollo, Delphi, 9
Terrorism, 95
Tesla, 16
Thirty Years' War (1618–48), 134
Thus Spoke Zarathustra (Nietzsche), 5
Tomasi di Lampedusa, Giuseppe, 11
Torture, 23, 30, 31, 96
Trademark laws, 18
Tragedy of the commons, 37
Transference, 98–99
Transformation
    7C sequence, 108
    workshops, 109, 118, 119
Trump, Donald, 8, 95
Trust, 43, 87, 102, 111, 120, 122
Trustworthiness, 7
Turf wars, 111, 120
Turgenev, Ivan, 74
Turkey, 95
Tutankhamen, Pharaoh of Egypt, 1
Twice-borns, 3–6, 9

U

United States
    astrology in, 131
    Trump administration, 8
Unsafe products, 23

V

Value-oriented education, 101
Van Gogh, Vincent, 115
Victimless crimes, 44, 50
Virgil, 81

Volkswagen, 43
Voltaire, 130
von Goethe, Johann Wolfgang, 123, 151

W

Wall Street (1987 film), 22
Wason, Peter, 127n4
Weber, Max, 93, 94, 99
Weltanschauung, 7, 85, 156
Whistleblowers, 50
White-collar crime
   corporate culture and, 51
   corporate psychopathy and, 48
   cost of, 43, 50
   deadliness, 43
   Fraud Triangle/Diamond, 46, 50
   greed and, 46
   narcissism and, 47
   prevention of, 49
   psychopathy and, 49
   self-control and, 47
   socio-demographics of, 42
Wiesel, Elie, 25

Wilson, Woodrow, 107
Witches, 129
Wizard of Lies, The (2017 film), 42
Wolf of Wall Street, 22
Workaholism, 57
Workshops, 60, 109–112, 118–121, 126
World War II, 24, 31
Wrath, 13, 14, 16, 17, 20

Y

Yachts, 42, 81, 82, 88, 96
Yakubets, Maksim, 22

Z

Zen Buddhism, 11, 131, 139
Zero-symbol incident, 136
Zimbardo, Philip, 26, 26n2, 27
Zitelmann, Rainer, 83, 84
Zodiac, 124, 128
Zodiac killer, 129
Zoteekos, 121, 122
Zuckerberg, Mark, 83

GPSR Compliance
The European Union's (EU) General Product Safety Regulation (GPSR) is a set of rules that requires consumer products to be safe and our obligations to ensure this.

If you have any concerns about our products, you can contact us on

ProductSafety@springernature.com

In case Publisher is established outside the EU, the EU authorized representative is:

Springer Nature Customer Service Center GmbH
Europaplatz 3
69115 Heidelberg, Germany

www.ingramcontent.com/pod-product-compliance
Lightning Source LLC
LaVergne TN
LVHW011006250326
834688LV00004B/108